PRAISE FOR DEEPER LEARNING THROUGH TECHNOLOGY: USING THE CLOUD TO INDIVIDUALIZE INSTRUCTION

This is a great book for all educators. Spending time to learn how to employ technology tools for the classroom, especially when they are simple and free, saves hours of time per week and ultimately makes teachers' lives much easier, so they can spend more time doing what they love—teaching.

Brett Kopf, Co-Founder
Remind.com

For teachers grappling with the rise of online learning in schools, this is a must read—a detailed nuts and bolts guide to classroom tools in the cloud.

Michael B. Horn, Co-Founder and
Director, Christensen Institute
Author of *Disrupting Class: How Disruptive
Innovation Will Change the Way the World Learns*

One of the most common complaints I hear from students is that their teachers don't understand how to effectively use technology to enhance learning. However, Ken Halla has become one of the most highly regarded teachers in our community as a result of his work engaging students in new ways, so much so that his trending hashtags on Twitter consistently inspire students to delve more deeply into course content outside of the classroom. I am so glad he has written this book to help other teachers and administrators learn from his successes.

Ryan McElveen, At-Large Member
Fairfax County (VA) School Board

For most of history, where you were born and your proximity to books, resources, and libraries were factors that impacted your potential for academic success. This is no longer true. In our lifetime, there has been a fundamental shift to this long-standing reality. Today our teachers and students have 1 billion libraries and all the world's information at our fingertips. Technology has integrated into the core of all our lives and into almost everything we do. In education, it is no longer a question of whether we integrate technology in education, it is a question of how we do it. What Ken Halla has done in Deeper Learning Through Technology *is lay out how teachers can integrate technology into their* ___ *take advantage of this new world we live in, but more impo*___

better meet the needs that students face today as they prepare to develop the knowledge, skills, and abilities they need to thrive in their futures. In this book, not only does Halla do a masterful job of covering all the important aspects, tools, and resources of education technology teachers need to understand, he supports what he highlights with real classroom examples and provides challenges teachers can take on as they master these skills. Whether you are a veteran to ed technology or just getting started, Halla's book will help you tailor learning to meet the needs of your students and take on new teaching methodologies and tools to help you create the learner-focused classroom you want to build! This is a must have resource for today's teachers!

Jaime Casap, Global Education Evangelist
Google

Technology is transforming the business of teaching and learning. Thankfully we have Ken Halla who provides here a timely guide to navigate this new digital classroom. Ken's resourceful guide is for every teacher who wants to steer into the new world of teaching and learning with confidence.

Dan Larsen, Social Studies Teacher
Stevenson High School
Co-Founder, CitizenU.org

Ken Halla is a teacher committed to improving his craft by learning and interacting with other educators. His dedication to enhancing instructional practice and meeting the needs of every student through the integration of technology is well documented in this book. It is a must read for any educator interested in meeting the needs of 21st century students.

John Kellogg, Superintendent
Westerville (OH) City School District

The author has made it easy for the teacher to work electronic devices into the classroom and prepare the students for a student-led classroom. The book is so organized that beginners can have success in a short amount of time. Students and teachers will love it.

Susan Harmon, Technology and Science Instructor
Neodesha Jr./Sr. High School
Neodesha, KS

This book provides a focus that is missing from most integration related resources. It focuses on changing instruction. Teachers will not be intimidated by the rationale and ideas the author presents. The examples are realistic, applicable, and easily reproducible by teachers.

John Lustig, Technology Director
Saint Peter Public Schools
St. Peter, MN

I am not just reading. I am learning on the spot. I can go to my classroom tomorrow and use information I learned about while reading. Our students love to use technology. Why not motivate them by using what they enjoy so much? This book will provide powerful information on how to engage your students with technology.

Tamara Daugherty, Third Grade Teacher
Lakeville Elementary
Apopka, FL

Need to help your students become a 21st century learner? Look no further! This book is all you need and you too will learn something new!

Gina Powell, Instructional Technology Resource Teacher
Essex County Public Schools
Tappahannock, VA

I am thrilled to have a copy of this book and want to get it into the hands of my principal, tech teacher and colleagues. It is a straight-forward, well-organized, and a smart approach to developing 21st century expertise in educators of every level. We need this book in my school system. If I had the power, I would order a copy for every employee and then set about forming PLNs for its use.

April Keck DeGennaro, Teacher
Peeples Elementary School
Fayetteville, GA

Deeper Learning Through Technology

This book is dedicated to these important people in my life.

My wife, Debbie, who is always supportive of my projects.

My kids, Madison, Alexandra, and Grant,
who often did their homework as Dad did his writing.

My grandfather Paul, who gave me my middle name
and who was the first teacher in my family. I only wish we could
have shared our teaching experiences with each other.

The thousands of students I have taught over the years. I love
teaching the content, but my students are the ones who drive me the
most and make me want to improve my craft continually.

Deeper Learning Through Technology

Using the Cloud to Individualize Instruction

Ken Halla

CORWIN
A SAGE Company

FOR INFORMATION:

Corwin
A SAGE Company
2455 Teller Road
Thousand Oaks, California 91320
(800) 233-9936
www.corwin.com

SAGE Publications Ltd.
1 Oliver's Yard
55 City Road
London EC1Y 1SP
United Kingdom

SAGE Publications India Pvt. Ltd.
B 1/I 1 Mohan Cooperative Industrial Area
Mathura Road, New Delhi 110 044
India

SAGE Publications Asia-Pacific Pte. Ltd.
3 Church Street
#10-04 Samsung Hub
Singapore 049483

A catalog record of this book is available from the Library of Congress.

ISBN 978-1-4833-4468-3

Executive Editor: Arnis Burvikovs
Associate Editor: Desirée A. Bartlett
Editorial Assistant: Andrew Olson
Production Editor: Amy Schroller
Copy Editor: Ellen Howard
Typesetter: C&M Digitals (P) Ltd.
Proofreader: Ellen Brink
Indexer: Judy Hunt
Cover Designer: Anupama Krishnan
Marketing Manager: Stephanie Trkay

15 16 17 18 19 10 9 8 7 6 5 4 3 2 1

Contents

Links for a Teacher's Guide to Student Self-Pacing in the Digital Classroom

Chapter 1. Our Changing Digital World

1. TED Talks *www.ted.com/*

2. Ken Robinson, Changing Education Paradigms *https://www.youtube.com/watch?v=zDZFcDGpL4U*

3. Smartphones, Tablets, and Computers
   a. Google Play *https://play.google.com/store*
   b. iTunes *https://www.apple.com/itunes/*

4. Choosing a Browser
   a. Google Chrome *https://www.google.com/intl/en_us/chrome/browser*
   b. Firefox *https://www.mozilla.org/en-US/firefox/new*
   c. Explorer *http://www.microsoft.com/en-us/download/internet-explorer.aspx*
   d. Safari *http://support.apple.com/downloads/#safari*
   e. Chromebooks *http://www.google.com/intl/en/chrome/devices*

5. Searching the Web: YouTube *http://youtube.com*

6. Cookies
   a. TED Presentation by Eli Parisen *http://www.youtube.com/watch?v=B8ofWFx525s&feature=player_embedded*
   b. DuckDuckGo *https://duckduckgo.com*

7. Citations Made Easy: EasyBib *http://www.easybib.com/*

8. Literate Digital Citizens: Project RED: *http://pearsonfoundation.org/downloads/ProjectRED_TheTechnolgyFactor.pdf*

Chapter 2. Teacher Collaboration:
Online Professional Learning Communities

1. Twitter *twitter.com*
   a. Cool Cat Teacher = @coolcatteacher *https://twitter.com/coolcatteacher*
   b. We Are Teachers = @WeAreTeachers *https://twitter.com/WeAreTeachers*
   c. Eric Sheninger = @E_Sheninger *https://twitter.com/NMHS_Principal*
   d. Richard Byrne = @rmbyrne *https://twitter.com/rmbyrne*
   e. Shelly Terrell = @ShellTerrell *https://twitter.com/ShellTerrell*
   f. Ken Halla = @kenhalla *https://twitter.com/kenhalla*
   g. Keeping Tweets With Storify *https://storify.com/*

2. Storify
   a. Storify website *https://storify.com*
   b. Storify tutorial, House Divided *https://www.youtube.com/watch?v=luZcU2E5cgI*

3. Hashtags
   a. Edudemic *http://www.edudemic.com/*
   b. 300+ Educational Hashtags *http://www.edudemic.com/twitter-hashtags-now/*
   c. Cybraryman *http://cybraryman.com/chats.html*
   d. #sschat *https://twitter.com/search?q=%23sschat&src=typd*
   e. #musechat *https://twitter.com/search?q=%23musechat%20&src=typd*
   f. #kinderchat *https://twitter.com/search?q=%23kinderchat%20&src=typd*
   g. #scichat *https://twitter.com/search?q=%23scichat&src=typd*
   h. #artsed *https://twitter.com/search?q=%23artsed%09&src=typd*
   i. #langchat *https://twitter.com/search?q=%23langchat&src=typd*
   j. #elemchat *https://twitter.com/search?q=%23elemchat&src=typd*

4. Google Plus Communities
   a. Google Plus *http://plus.google.com*
   b. Google for Education *https://plus.google.com/+GoogleforEducation/posts*
   c. Edudemic *https://plus.google.com/+Edudemic/posts*
   d. Education Week *https://plus.google.com/+EducationWeek/posts*
   e. Education Revolution *https://plus.google.com/communities/104214480154015052148*
   f. Google Certified Teachers *https://plus.google.com/communities/117648313735580056690*
   g. Google Apps for Education *https://plus.google.com/communities/101802680117484972712*
   h. NeedToMeet *http://www.needtomeet.com/*

5. Educator Blogs
   a. Edublogs *http://edublogs.org/community/*
   b. Edudemic *http://www.edudemic.com/teacher-blogs/*

Source: Spencer, 2013.

Chapter 5. Interactive Assignments

f. SMOG Index *http://en.wikipedia.org/wiki/SMOG*

g. Fry Readability Formula *http://en.wikipedia.org/wiki/Fry_readability_formula*

h. Coleman-Lieu Index *http://en.wikipedia.org/wiki/Coleman%E2%80%93 Liau_index*

3. Learning Styles

a. Felder and Silverman *http://www.engr.ncsu.edu/learningstyles/ilsweb .html*

b. Felder's Index of Learning Styles *http://www4.ncsu.edu/unity/lockers/ users/f/felder/public/ILSpage.html*

c. Bloom's Digital Taxonomy Wheel and Knowledge Dimension *http:// eductechalogy.org/swfapp/blooms/wheel/engage.swf*

d. Faking It

    i. Fakebook *http://www.classtools.net/FB/home-page*

    ii. FakeTweet *http://faketweetbuilder.com/*

    iii. FakeText *http://faketweetbuilder.com/*

    iv. Russell Tarr @russeltarr *https://twitter.com/russeltarr*

e. Free Textbook Resources: Hippocampus *http://www.hippocampus.org*

f. Schoolhouse Rock:

    i. I'm Just a Bill on Capitol Hill *https://www.youtube.com/watch?v=F FroMQlKiag*

    ii. How a Bill Really Becomes a Law: What Schoolhouse Rock Missed *https://www.youtube.com/watch?v=QH0Hl31vdF4*

g. iBook Author *https://www.apple.com/ibooks-author/*

h. Rubric: Rubistar *http://rubistar.4teachers.org/index.php*

Chapter 6. Student Collaboration: Engaging Students With Mobile Learning

1. Changing Teaching Styles in a Digital Classroom

a. Grooveshark *http://grooveshark.com*

b. iTunes *https://www.apple.com/itunes/*

c. Google Play *https://play.google.com/store?hl=en*

d. Free Conference Call *https://www.freeconferencecall.com*

e. Face to Faith *http://tonyblairfaithfoundation.org/projects/facetofaith*

2. Cooperative Learning Using Twitter

a. TweetChat *http://tweetchat.com/*

b. Twitterfall *http://twitterfall.com*

c. @kenhalla *http://twitter.com/kenhalla*

d. @HideChat *https://twitter.com/HideChat*

3. Other Tools to Engage Students
   a. Quick Response Generator Karem Erkan *http://keremerkan.net/qr-code-and-2d-code-generator/*
   b. Blackboard *http://www.blackboard.com*
   c. Edmodo *https://www.edmodo.com*
   d. Moodle *https://moodle.org*
   e. Google Sites *http://sites.google.com*
   f. Remind *http://remind.com/*
   g. Tinyurl *http://tinyurl.com*
   h. Bitly *https://bitly.com*

Chapter 7. Formative and Summative Assessment of Student Learning

1. Preparing the Formative and Summative Evaluations
   a. Google Hangouts *https://www.google.com/+/learnmore/hangouts/*
   b. Free Conference Call *https://www.freeconferencecall.com*
   c. Twitter *http://twitter.com*
   d. TodaysMeet *http://todaysmeet.com/*
   e. Flubaroo *http://www.flubaroo.com*
   f. Poll Everywhere *http://www.polleverywhere.com/*
   g. Cel.ly *http://cel.ly/*
   h. Quizlet *http://quizlet.com/*

Chapter 8. Looking Forward Into the Present

(no links)

Preface

PURPOSE AND RATIONALE

Deeper Learning Through Technology is a practical guide for teachers to help them to further integrate technology into their classrooms to better meet student needs. The chapters will highlight practical applications that you can employ right away or use as a guide to implement over the school year. Ideally it will be a stepping stone for you to become your own digital muse so that you will be able to find your own resources, improve your classroom, and one day write a book for me to read on how I, too, can change my craft. Be forewarned, though, this is not about integrating technology for the sake of technology, but rather about how to use technology to more effectively individualize learning for your students.

> This is not about integrating technology for the sake of technology, but rather about how to use technology to more effectively individualize learning for your students.

This book is written for teachers who realize that their classes have been infiltrated by technology with or without their permission. Just a few years ago, very few students had cell phones. Now most not only have smartphones, but often prefer using them to laptops or even tablets. One of the most ubiquitous devices in our society—the iPhone—did not come out until 2007, and the iPad has been available only since 2010. Since the iPad, there has been a proliferation of cheaper tablets and laptops on the market, prompting more students to want to bring a myriad of different Internet-based devices to your classroom. This is in addition to all of the devices schools are purchasing. This book aims to help prepare you for these changes. It is meant as a practical learning manual for **teachers** and **content administrators** who are struggling to teach an ever-growing curriculum and skill set as efficiently as possible.

> The goal of this book is to demonstrate and guide second-order change in classrooms.

The goal of this book is to demonstrate and guide second-order change in classrooms. An example of first-order change is when a teacher uses technology to do something that she used to do with paper. Having students write on digitized paper might help the student better prepare for the digitized workforce, but doesn't necessarily make for better learning. On the other hand, second-order change involves utilizing technology and new resources to accomplish tasks and goals that have previously been impossible, such as collaborating with experts in fields of study or having students collaborate on projects with other students from around the country and around the world.

A BRIEF OVERVIEW

This book is broken into two parts. Part I: The Teacher as Leader of the Digital Classroom and Part II: The Self-Paced Student.

Part I explores the teacher as a lifelong learner and offers tips on how teachers can pursue their professional learning on an ongoing basis. It will serve as a foundation to give teachers the tools to continue the learning process, even as the needs of their students continue to change and the digital environment develops further. To that end, the first half of this book can be used by any educator, be she or he a principal, central administrator, or a teacher to expand his or her learning on a daily basis.

Part II specifically looks at pacing classes to meet the needs of individual learners, acknowledging that not all students will learn at the same speed. The book will further be broken up into the following chapters.

Part I: The Teacher as Leader of the Digital Classroom

Part I will introduce educators to many Internet tools that can be utilized to improve not only student learning but also their own professional learning. Ideally, these online tools will help bring about the second-order changes in teaching and learning that we as educators should be aiming for.

Chapter 1. Our Changing Digital World. This chapter details the responsibilities of teachers and students in the digital age. Students need to focus on creating positive digital footprints, and educators have to be aware of their mandate to protect pupils. The chapter concludes with examples of changes that technology can facilitate such as placing student work online (first-order) or fundamentally changing the way teachers teach (second-order).

Chapter 2. Teacher Collaboration: Online Professional Learning Communities. One of the most profound and widespread changes in education in the last decade has been the advent of professional learning communities (PLCs). Unfortunately these have been largely limited to content teams within schools. This chapter will show readers how to expand their professional learning communities beyond the school doors across the state, the country, and even the world. By using technology to effect second-order change, teachers will learn how to collaborate with educators they might never meet but who can profoundly enrich their classrooms.

Chapter 3. Storing and Sharing in the Cloud. This chapter will instruct teachers on how to store ideas in the cloud so that the information can be shared with others. By storing information in the cloud, it is accessible at any time on any Internet-based device. Teachers will also learn how to facilitate collaboration between students—within their own classroom, with students from other schools, even with students from around the world.

Part II: The Self-Paced Student

This section makes the case that students learn more effectively at their own pace and offers strategies to help teachers design individualized instruction for their students.

Chapter 4. The Self-Paced Anchor: Flipping the Classroom. This chapter will explain how teachers can deliver content information to students to be consumed at home at their own pace while spending class time providing interactive lessons. This chapter builds on Chapter 3 by detailing the many ways Google Drive can be used to facilitate the flipped classroom.

Chapter 5. Interactive Assignments. This section looks at student abilities, the reading level of materials, and the way material is presented. It builds on Chapter 4's flipped videos by showing teachers how to build interactive lessons, with the teacher serving as the facilitator of interactive student learning. To do this will mean looking at student abilities and at Bloom's taxonomy to develop higher-level student assignments.

Chapter 6. Student Collaboration: Engaging Students With Mobile Learning. This chapter will explore the benefits both of student collaboration as well as how to enhance it with mobile technology. Collaborative learning can take place both face-to-face within the classroom, and also in virtual time and space in the cloud.

Chapter 7. Formative and Summative Assessment of Student Learning. Teachers will learn how to conduct formative and summative assessments using online tools. The chapter will also explore test review resources (made by other teachers and students) stored in the cloud.

Chapter 8. Looking Forward Into the Present. This chapter summarizes the major components of the book and ends with a look at Mooresville, North Carolina, a school system that embraces technology and that, as a result, has seen dramatic improvement in its test scores.

WHY YOU SHOULD BUY THIS BOOK

This book will help you bring a revolution in learning to your classroom! You will learn how to

- **Expand your Professional Learning Community (PLC)** beyond your school or district's boundaries. This will help you generate amazing new ideas with the advice of the many online leaders you will find by following the suggestions in this book.
- **Individualize instruction,** tailoring learning to the pace and needs of each student. You will be better able to differentiate and also have more one-on-one time with each student.
- **Tackle new tech tools** so that you can create a learner-centered, self-paced classroom. You will find chapters filled with easy to understand bullet points that will help you ease into new tools or explore previously known tools in more depth.
- **Find real classroom examples** that show you how you too can implement the strategies described in the book.
- **Be challenged.** Each chapter contains five Educator Challenges to help you focus on changing your classroom as slowly or as quickly as you feel appropriate.

This book is meant to be used two ways. For those with little experience in implementing Internet-based learning, it can be used to incorporate bite-sized chunks of change. For those who already have been making the shift into digital education and are ready to dive in headfirst, this book can fundamentally change the way you are teaching. So let's get going!

Acknowledgments

A year ago I was asked by Corwin if I would write a book. I had been thinking of such an endeavor for some time, so I knocked out the first draft in just three months. But then I spent the next nine drafting and redrafting. During that time, Desirée Bartlett was an extremely thoughtful editor who, thankfully, set strong deadlines and deserves most of the credit for the quality of this book. It was at times frustrating for both of us but, ultimately, a very rewarding learning experience.

Thanks also to my developmental editor, Frank Franz, for not only reading my book and giving me numerous suggestions but also for letting me bounce ideas off him for the last decade.

Finally thank you to the many peer reviewers who took the time to give me numerous suggestions for improving this book.

PUBLISHER'S ACKNOWLEDGMENTS

Corwin gratefully acknowledges the contributions of the following reviewers:

Tamara Daugherty, Third-Grade Teacher
Lakeville Elementary
Apopka, FL

Susan Harmon, Middle School Teacher
Neodesha Jr./Sr. High School
Neodesha, KS

Alexis Ludewig, Supervisor of Student Teachers
University of Wisconsin–Oshkosh
Oshkosh, WI

John Lustig, Technology Director
Saint Peter Public Schools
St. Peter, MN

Dr. Gary L. Willhite, Professor
University of Wisconsin–La Crosse
La Crosse, WI

About the Author

Ken Halla has been teaching high school social studies since 1991, during which time he has taught virtually the entire catalog of offerings in his department, from world history to government. He has also been an advanced placement coordinator and department chair. Not limited to brick-and-mortar teaching, he has taught online classes since 2001. Halla affirms that "teaching is my passion because it lets me work with energizing young adults and continue to learn new information. All these years later, I still love going to school every morning."

In addition to teaching high school students, Halla has also taught government classes at George Mason University for a decade and has led many teacher in-service classes, both online and in person for middle and high school teachers. His self-designed "Enhancing the Social Studies Classroom with Technology" has become one of the most popular offerings in his home county, Fairfax—the thirteenth largest in the United States. Teachers from kindergarten through high school and from all disciplines, including technology specialists, sign up for the professional development class because Halla tailors the classes to each educator's classroom needs. He serves on the College Board's 6–12th grade Advisory Panel for Social Studies, and his four blogs (Economics Teachers, US Government Teachers, US History Teachers, and World History Teachers) are among the most visited teacher sites in the United States, with 65,000+ hits a month. Halla's endeavors inside and outside the classroom have been featured on ABC and NBC news and in the National Education Association's *Today* magazine, *Education Week,* and the *Washington Post.*

Halla spent most of his formative years living abroad in Belgium, France, and Iran, and he still enjoys traveling overseas with his family. Halla's other passion is running. He was a four-time All-American athlete at the

College of William and Mary and later a finalist at the US Olympic Track and Field Trials. He has two master's degrees, in teaching and international relations, and a PhD in political science from George Washington University and is a National Board Certified teacher. When not teaching, he enjoys being with his three children, Madison, Alexandra, and Grant, and his wife, Debbie.

If you are interested in having Ken Halla come to your school for an in-service, you can contact him at *kenhalla@gmail.com.*

To see more of his writing, follow his blogs:

Economics Teachers: economicsteachersblog.blogspot.com/

US Government Teachers: usgovteducatorsblog.blogspot.com/

US History Teachers: ushistoryeducatorblog.blogspot.com/

World History Teachers: worldhistoryeducatorsblog.blogspot.com/

Part I

The Teacher as Leader of the Digital Classroom

1 Our Changing Digital World

- Take a tour of the Internet
- Learn how become a more responsible digital citizen
- Learn tools for implementing second-order change

TOURING THE INTERNET

This chapter will help you understand a little bit more about how the Internet works. We will look into its many benefits as well as some of its pitfalls and, most importantly, how you can protect yourself and your students when using the numerous resources in this book.

Over one hundred years ago, my grandfather spent the year after high school working as a teacher to trying to earn money for college. He worked in a typical one-room schoolhouse. Between his teaching tenure and the start of my career, about the only thing that changed was moving from giving students slate writing tablets to giving them pencils and paper. The one-room schoolhouse was replaced by many one-room schoolhouses—all in the same building. But other than a few innovative programs or some coordination between content fields, there have been few significant changes in the way we teach—until the past few years. This book begins with technology offering us the tools to overturn the traditional educational system.

One of the best places to find a collection of educationally disruptive ideas online is the TED Talks site. TED Talks are gatherings of innovators who tell or show their latest thoughts or computer applications. The talks are recorded and put on the TED Talks site, garnering millions of views a year. One of the most popular TED Talks stars is Sir Ken Robinson, whose talk "Changing Education Paradigms" puts forth the notion that our schools are relics, of the Industrial Revolution. He affirms that schools were started to train managers to work in lockstep, with little concern for individualization and ability. Those who can master content at the same age as everyone else are considered "good students," and those who cannot are left on the educational dustheap. But for every educational failure, there are plenty of people and students who, given more time, can be superstars if offered personalized pacing. We all know, though, that students often are the sum of their previous years. Those who do well, continue to do so. Malcolm Gladwell calls this the accumulative advantage, which he suggests is simply based on those who are the oldest in a class doing the best. ("Is Your Birthday an Advantage in School?" 2008) For example, I have an October birthday and so was older than all but a few of my peers every year of my education. Gladwell contends that I had a cognitive advantage simply because my body was more physically advanced and so, over time, this advantage built on itself.

As you read this book, think of how much or little the education system in the United States has changed or been disruptive since the Industrial Revolution. You will notice three strands throughout the book: (1) seeing the teacher as a lifelong learner (Part I), (2) individualizing instruction for each student (Part II), and (3) weaving technology throughout teaching (the whole book). The first half of the book, "Teacher as Learner," will help you to realize that you are not alone. Whether you are the only one in your school using this book or the entire staff is using it, you need to realize that there are far more resources beyond your school door. The commitment to expand your Professional Learning Community (PLC) must go beyond your insular world and can be done with a minimal commitment each week. A PLC is a like-minded group of educators that meets regularly to discuss ways to teach, ways to assess learning, and various other professional learning concerns.

> The commitment to expand your Professional Learning Community (PLC) must go beyond your insular world and can be done with a minimal commitment each week.

The second half of the book will concentrate on the fact that students progress at different speeds. As the father of twins, this has been apparent to me since my daughters were infants. Letting them strive at their own speed and focusing on their individual talents has been a particular focus of my wife's and mine their entire lives. You will be offered techniques to master maximizing the time you spend with each of your students, giving them as little or as much time as they need to learn the content. This will go against most people's thoughts of a normal classroom; however, the book is not meant to change your classroom in a few weeks, but rather in bite-sized chunks. As with your students, you should progress at the rate that best suits you, your PLC, and your school. Undoubtedly there will be a few teachers who will progress more quickly and can, in turn, help their colleagues develop as well.

The third strand is technology. Without technology, it would be virtually impossible to work across schools, counties, states, and countries to find new peers and ideas. Indeed it would be almost a chaotic situation in your class if you were to have thirty different students in five or six places in the curriculum. Now, however, with the Internet and the proliferation of inexpensive devices, the self-paced student has become possible. The Internet can be used as a tool to improve the way your students learn, synthesize, and retain information.

To get started, some background information might be useful. For some, the information in this chapter might be completely new, while for others it can serve as a quick refresher course. What you pay attention to very likely will depend on your role in school. Administrators have to be more concerned with the legal and financial issues surrounding online strategies, while teachers will tend to focus more on the parts relevant to instruction.

Smartphones, Tablets, and Laptops

At the ripe young age of fifty, I am old enough to remember going to the Honeywell building near my childhood home and seeing a room full of computers driven by large reels that had far less power than your child's basic school calculator. We now carry around computers in our pockets, which we know as smartphones. These devices can make phone calls, send and receive texts, and access the Internet. Since smartphones and tablets cannot perform all of the tasks of a laptop, there are millions of applications (apps) available that can be downloaded onto smartphones and tablets. Apps are self-contained programs or pieces of software designed to fulfill a particular purposes. They are limited in scope but are usually very useful for their intended purposes. To download apps, either for purchase or for free, visit the online app store via your device. If you have an Apple device, access the iTunes store online; and if you have an Android (Google) product, also known as an Android device, access the Google Play store.

Visit http://bit.ly/digitalclassroomteacherguide to access live links.

Most of us do not complete the bulk of our work on a smartphone but instead choose a desktop or laptop computer for more complex tasks. Desktops are computers that generally stay on your desk's top—hence the name—as they are too large to put into a bag and carry around easily. Laptops can be folded in two, put in a case, and moved from place to place. If you follow all the steps in this book, a laptop or a tablet is all you will ever need again—no paper, no filing cabinets, no clutter.

Tablets generally have screens that are smaller than laptop screens (7–10 inches on average) and have no separate area for typing other than the screen. Tablets have the advantage of being smaller than laptops, but they do not yet have all of the functionality of laptops. While they can be very handy and can complete many of the functions of a laptop, the smaller screen often means that people additionally purchase a keyboard to go along with it—effectively creating a laptop. To perform daily tasks on tablets, users must download several apps onto their devices, as they would with a smartphone. Ironically smartphones are now getting larger, blurring the difference between them and tablets.

The Internet—What Is It Exactly?

It is always important to give students a sense of context to facilitate understanding. Therefore, students' ability to better utilize the Internet would be aided if they better understood its origins and how it works. So before proceeding, it might be helpful to explore what is meant by the Internet. We all use the term many times daily, but do we really know what it means? When the Internet started is debatable. By 1968 there were four US military-sponsored computers called ARPANET that were connected to one another. Signals could be sent back and forth between computers, and they even had the ability to have one computer take over and control another. ARPANET used "Network Protocol Control," which essentially set the rules, or protocol, for the connections between the computers (Sterling, 1993). As more and more computers were added, literally a network of networks—an internet—was developed. Since there was no standard internet protocol until 1983, the year ARPANET converted to this system, 1983 is viewed by many as the birthday of the Internet ("A Brief History of the Internet," 2013; "History of the Internet," n.d.). When you send a message between computers, you are doing so from an Internet device (laptop, smartphone, or tablet) with its own personal Internet Protocol (IP) address.

There are many people who have helped in the creation of the modern Internet, but Tim Berners-Lee is often credited as being its "father." He was the first one to use Hypertext Transfer Protocol (HTTP), the current language of the Internet, which he "invented" in November 1989. We are now working on implementing the fifth version of the Internet, called HTML5. It seeks to bring together accepted protocols as well as to develop a platform that will make it easier to use tablets and smartphones by calling for fewer downloads or plug-ins so that more and more items will be accessible in a browser. In other words, we will be moving more and more to cloud computing (defined below).

But what is meant by the Internet in a physical sense? We know the Internet started with several computers networked together. Now it is a series of wires, fiber optics, satellite connections, and even thick cords running under the Atlantic and Pacific Oceans that connect all computers with Internet access to one another. Each computer on which an Internet page is held is called a server. Since your computer is probably not a server, it is likely connected to an Internet provider such as Cox Communications or Comcast.

When you attempt to visit a website, the signal is broken up into thousands of bits. The bits travel with instructions, including the IP address of the website, in what is known as a packet (World Science Festival, 2012). Once the signal is received, the Internet protocol is again used to follow the rules to put the bits back together again. There are a series of "Internet exchange points" through which all of these bits must travel (Data Centers Canada, 2011). One of the largest hub centers is located in Loudoun County, Virginia, and covers 400,000 square feet of space—a total of seven football fields. All told the there are 40 centers in Loudoun covering four million square feet (seventy football fields) with over six more projected by 2021 (Censer, 2011). Other major hub centers in the United States are located in Los Angeles, New Jersey, New York City, and Silicon Valley. Through these centers travel most of the work that you and your students will be conducting between all the various servers and computers that will be helping all of you do your work.

The Cloud

As computer scientists have made the Internet more efficient, people have been starting to store less and less on their home computers and more and more in "the cloud." This means that the work you do on computers and devices is moving onto shared computer servers that are accessible on any device with an Internet connection. These servers are essentially like the guts of your computer but are stacked one on top of the other with a sliver of space between each. They reside in football field-length buildings often near water sources that are used to keep the temperatures of the buildings at a cool sixty-seven degrees. Hosting data has already become big business for many companies. For example, Amazon, in 2012, was estimated to have over 450,000 servers storing information for thousands of companies (Miller, 2012). If everything is stored on processors in giant data centers (the cloud), then the device you use to access it will not need nearly as much processing power as it has needed in the past. More importantly, you will not be dependent on one particular device. The advantage of this is that you will need just an Internet device that is fast enough to access your stored data. As cloud computing spreads, it will mean you will be able to purchase cheaper Internet portals and therefore be able to do more and more work on tablets and smartphones.

Two fears that are frequently raised regarding switching to cloud computing are hacking and reliability. If I store my files in the cloud, will they be easier for hackers to access? If I store my photographs, videos, and files in the cloud, will I risk losing them forever? The truth is that any device connected to the Internet is susceptible to hacking. Hackers, though, can access anyone's home computer if it is connected to the Internet just as they can access information banks stored online. When a home computer crashes for good, everything stored on that computer may be forever lost. In contrast, information stored in the cloud is backed up on several servers so, if one fails, another will take its place. Therefore, while we may perceive information stored on our personal computers as safer, the truth is just the opposite.

Browsers

To access information from a variety of devices (a benefit of cloud computing), you can save your work in a browser. Browsers—or Internet portals—in order of popularity include <u>Google's Chrome</u> (53 percent), <u>Firefox</u> (28 percent), Microsoft's Explorer (13 percent) and Apple's <u>Safari</u> (4 percent) ("Browser Statistics," 2012). From the browser, we often use a search engine to look up information. The three leading search engines are Google (65 percent), <u>Baidu</u> (8 percent), and Yahoo (5 percent). If you haven't heard of Baidu, it is because it is China's leading search engine and looks conspicuously like Google's search page (Sullivan, 2013). As we move further into HTML5, it will be possible to do more and more work on the browser without having to download anything onto personal devices. This means faster speed and cheaper devices for you and your students. Soon schools will no longer be providing devices for most of their students as most parents will not mind their children bringing $200 laptops or tablets just as many do not mind them bringing $200 smartphones to school now. Already there are several companies producing $200–$250 laptops that are essentially just processors for browsers. In 2013, 22 percent of US school districts were using such devices, specifically <u>Chromebooks</u> (Bort, 2013).

Search Engines

As you read through this book, you will be using a search engine to find each of the technology tools mentioned in the book. Here are some search engine tips you might not know:

- Simple is better than complicated. If you know some of the exact words, put them in quotes and make them as descriptive as possible. For example, if you want to see if someone has uploaded a PowerPoint on Macbeth online, just type "Macbeth ppt" or "Macbeth PowerPoint" or "book summary Macbeth PowerPoint."
- If you write a math problem in the search box and press enter, the search engine will solve it for you.
- Enter "weather 22310" to get information on the weather in the 22310 zip code.
- Type in any word along with "definition" to obtain a definition.
- Chrome offers users the option of clicking on the tiny microphone beside the search box allowing you to speak your search terms rather than having to type them.
- You can find many more search tricks by typing "browser tricks" + the name of the search engine you are using

Another place to do a search is YouTube.com, which was started independently in 2005 and was purchased by Google for $1.85 billion the next year. Although once taboo in schools, YouTube has now become an important place for both teachers and students alike to grow. According to YouTube, one hundred hours of video are uploaded each minute, so there is something for almost every lesson you will teach ("Statistics," 2013). As an example of YouTube's usefulness, my daughter learned several art projects simply by exploring YouTube videos. You can also search for how to perform a mathematical function, how to serve a volleyball, and how to write a sonnet—you will find it all there. Be careful, though, because as with any research endeavor, you may not always find what you want on the first try, and not all of what you find will meet your needs in the classroom.

When you come across the mention of an Internet site in this book, go to a browser, type in the name of the website in the search bar, and you should be able to find it easily. You also should be aware that when you

When you come across the mention of an Internet site in this book go to a browser, type in the name of the website in the search bar, and you should be able to find it easily.

search for terms in a browser, cookies are being left on your Internet device so that the browser can better help you find exactly what you need on subsequent attempts. What, say you, is a cookie?

Cookies You Don't Want to Eat

Developed by Lou Montulli in 1994 when he worked for the then-world-leading browser Netscape, cookies help direct what we see on the Internet. Cookies are being downloaded on your laptop all the time and are collected by the web browsers you use. Essentially, they are individual identification numbers that a website assigns your computer as it collects information on how you used their page. Even apps you might add to your browsers or smartphone often collect this information—which is why they can be free, as they might sell your information to a group that is trying to reach people like you with similar interests and search patterns.

When you are searching the Internet you are utilizing an algorithm. This algorithm is a very long mathematical equation that helps you find the information you need. It is aided in part by the cookies on your Internet device that help direct searches to match not only your queries but your needs, based on what sites you have already used.

Let me give you an example. I recently visited the Virginia Republican and Democratic Party websites as part of my research for my students, and within one day I started getting ads for a lieutenant gubernatorial candidate that the microdata thought I might like to select in an upcoming primary. The browser had connected the fact that I love educational technology to the fact that the candidate was the former technology czar for both my former governor and Barack Obama. The good news is that more often than not, you see ads that match your interests, but the drawback is that you may not be led beyond your own limited interests. Author Eli Pariser argues in his book, *The Filter Bubble* (2011), and in his TED Talks presentation of the same name, that the news we hear and read is being increasingly limited only to the sources with which we tend to agree. He adds that this limitation is having a harmful impact on our democracy since it is giving people only what they want to hear rather than alternative modes of thought or points of view. To counter this limiting trend during your online experience, you can choose periodically to clean out the cookies on your Internet devices and browsers by going to a search engine and searching for "how to clean out cookies." But be forewarned that cookies allow your favorite websites to appear after you have written just a few letters, and these automatic populators will disappear when your cookies are deleted. If you want to try cookie-free searching, visit the search engine <u>DuckDuckGo</u>, which does not work off of any cookies and therefore offers you a search based off of a blind algorithm.

QR Codes

This book will include many recommendations for Internet sites. Most of these can easily be found by using a search engine. You will also see QR codes that will lead you to a list containing all of the live links. In each chapter of this book, you will see a black-and-white pixelated box (like the image below.). These are Quick Response or QR codes. The QR codes in this book all lead to the online document where you will find live links to the online resources and websites mentioned in this book.

To "read" a QR code, you will need a smartphone or tablet and a QR Reader.

- Download a free QR reader (there are many) on your smartphone or tablet from the iTunes or Google Play store.
- Once it has been loaded, tap the app and you will be able to view the QR square in the book via your device's camera lens. When you position your tablet or phone over the QR code, make sure that the QR code fits completely within the framed box on your device's screen. When this happens, the phone display will shake slightly and a website link—known as a URL—will appear with a button asking if you would like to visit the site. Click "ok" and your device will open the website.

In Chapter 6 we will discuss ways to use QR generators in your classroom.

In addition to using the QR codes, you can also access the live link document by visiting this site: http://bit.ly/ digitalclassroomteacherguide

BECOMING RESPONSIBLE DIGITAL CITIZENS

Just as we are expected to follow certain norms and rules in the "real world," so too must we practice good digital citizenship online. Since most of what we access on the Internet is beyond our control to modify or censor, we have to teach our students to be smart stewards when using the Internet and teach them ways to avoid the pitfalls they may encounter when using the Internet.

Visit http://bit.ly/digitalclassroomteacherguide to access live links.

The website *Digital Citizenship: Using Technology Appropriately* (n.d.) has nine elements that the authors want teachers to consider when using the Internet in class. You might want to discuss them with your school leaders and combine them with your school rules, if you have not done so already. A few of these will be discussed in the following sections.

Not every one of your students has access to the Internet, or if they do, they might be sharing one Internet device with multiple people. This means that when you use the Internet in your classroom, you should be flexible regarding due dates—without allowing some students to take advantage of your largess. Lobby for longer library hours and classroom laptops. Help your students locate public libraries and youth centers nearby that have free access. While ability will dictate speed for student learning, occasionally so will student access. But do not fall prey to those who say you should not plan lessons around the Internet if not all of your students have access. Students who do not have access to the Internet at home are in much greater need of these assignments if they are going to compete in a world that is entirely online. If they are not taught at home or in your classroom, then where will they learn?

Norms of digital communication and etiquette are important online. Your students are texting and using Twitter to communicate, and they need to be reminded that all messages can be seen by school officials, curators of websites, and third party players who may want to bully them. Both you and your students should be aware that school rules often apply to all online activity if it negatively impacts students in your school. Students need to be careful and never send messages that they would not mind everyone seeing if made public. If bullying is done on Twitter, it can be seen by school officials. Even if it was done at home, it still has an impact on student learning, and it might merit school punishment. Students have a hard time grasping this and, therefore, need frequent reminders.

Citing Sources

As you utilize the Internet to conduct research on search engines, you will find information that you'll want to use in your own writing and projects. Part of being a responsible digital citizen is giving credit where credit is due. Learning how (and teaching your students) to correctly cite sources of information found on the Internet is an essential component of responsible citizenry. As a teacher, you will need to stress over and over again that work borrowed from others must be correctly cited at all times.

Once a site is found by you or your students, it is important to give credit where it is due. EasyBib is a simple, user-friendly tool that will create properly formatted citations for you.

The Free Automatic Bibliography and Citation Generator

Save time by creating a Works Cited page instantly in MLA, APA, or Chicago!

| Website | Book | Newspaper | Journal | Database | All 59 options |

Manual entry Help   **MLA (free!)** APA Chicago/Turabian

Cite a website by entering its URL or by searching for it.   Cite this

Copy and paste the URL in the "Cite this" box and press enter. Depending on the site, you may have to enter the author's name and the date of publication manually, but all else is generally done for you. Once you have filled in the requested information, simply push the button at the bottom of the page asking for the citation and it will be written out for you in proper format including the day the citation was created.

You can also use EasyBib to make citations for images. Simply right click on the image and click on "copy URL" to get the link for any image.

Digital Laws: FERPA, COPPA, and CIPA

A good digital citizen knows the relevant laws. Teachers and administrators should most definitely know them! Students have to be made aware that their actions are creating a "digital footprint," much of which will be available on the Internet for years to come. Future employers will use the Internet to locate your students' lives online, and students need to know that pictures of crude behavior or poor word choices may come back to haunt them years later.

To help protect your students, particularly those younger than thirteen, digital laws have been developed by the federal government. When a teacher is put in front of a group of students, they are usually going to follow that leader and assume all is right with the various websites being utilized. So, to protect our children, there are three laws with which you should be familiar: (1) the Family Educational Rights and Privacy Act (FERPA), (2) the Children's Online Protection Act (COPPA), and (3) the Children's Internet Protection Act (CIPA).

FERPA, the oldest of the three laws, enacted in 1972, stipulates that parents and guardians should have access to their children's records and requires that schools obtain permission from parents before allowing student records to be seen by others. In regard to the digital classroom, FERPA can sometimes pose a tricky problem but certainly not one that can't be overcome. It's simply important to know what you can and cannot ask of

Visit http://bit.ly/digitalclassroomteacherguide to access live links.

your students. If you require students to go to a particular website to make a school presentation, it might be construed that you are releasing information to a third party without parental permission. Therefore, to comply with the law, it is important that you offer students alternatives to websites that are not protected by your school's servers or by a third party that has been contracted by your school district. School districts will often contract with companies to build a walled garden for a program to protect students. When not using these protected spaces, take precautions to ensure that you are not violating the law. Since so many websites and online tools require users to input an e-mail address and personal data, school systems run the risk of losing control of student data to third parties and, therefore, might be violating FERPA rights. Some sites allow teachers to create a unique class site, which students can use anonymously. That scenario would meet the requirements of FERPA because students are not giving away their personal information to others. Keeping the law in mind, make sure you always give students a choice as to whether or not to use the site, and offer viable alternatives. For instance, you can require students to make flashcards, but you must give them the choice of creating digital ones or paper-based ones. Complying with FERPA becomes easier as students get older.

Closely related to FERPA is COPPA, which requires a website collecting any information from children younger than thirteen to comply with certain federal regulations such as seeking parental permission when it knowingly targets minors. Websites such as Blackboard, which allows schools to put up assignments online, or Google Apps for Education (GAE) have built protected walls around their sites that require a login and password to enter. It is often assumed that schools have looked into the protections afforded by a website that might be used by a student and have received guarantees of protection of student data that is accessible in the cloud. COPPA was updated in 2010 to include protecting students' location, videos, image, voice, and even the use of cookies ("Security and Privacy of Cloud Computing," 2013).

Lastly, CIPA was passed in 2000, mandating that schools and libraries use filters to protect minors from online obscenities. If schools and libraries do not install the filters, they will be denied the "E-Rate" discounts for access to the Internet that can save them considerable amounts of money. Therefore, while filters are not mandated, most libraries will undoubtedly choose to comply with CIPA.

Higher Levels of Learning

Teachers who are good digital citizens realize that there is more to using the Internet with students than just protecting them online. It is equally important to ensure that Internet usage serves the purpose of deepening their learning. A study called <u>Project RED</u> looked at how digital literacy was being handled in our schools and contended that it should not be done just to replace paper but instead to take the learning to a higher level—thus making your students even better digital citizens (Greaves, Hayes, Wilson, Gielniak, & Peterson, 2010). Taking learning to a higher level is a very important point of this book. The first half of the book will offer teachers some tools to put lessons and assignments online, and the second half will help teachers take students to higher levels of learning by using online tools and resources.

Project RED (Greaves et al., 2010) looked at 997 schools in 47 states and the District of Columbia to see the impact of the digital learning environment. The report found that in schools where students all had digital devices (known as 1:1—one device for every student), test scores went up while dropout rates went down. The report emphasized that for the introduction of technology to be effective, instruction must also be meaningful. Project RED identified two levels of change—"first-order change" and "second-order change"—stressing that teachers and administrators should strive for second-order change if they want to improve student learning.

An example of first-order change would be when a teacher requires students to submit work online. This might save time that could be used for more direct instruction, but it is not necessarily changing instruction in any meaningful way. Whether assignments are on paper or submitted online, they still very likely reflect a similar quality of work. In contrast, second-order changes occur when technology allows for innovations that could not happen without it. For example, a teacher can assign students to watch an online video lecture (flipped video) for homework, visit and review several websites, and then collaborate with fellow students by commenting on the video and sites on one collective online document housed in the cloud. There are several second-order changes included in this scenario. (1) Placing the lecture online allows students to watch it at their own pace, stopping and starting the video or watching it several times until the material is understood. (2) Collaborating online means that students can work together regardless of where they physically happen to be (home, school, library, etc.). Both uses of technology (online video lecture and online collaborative document) allow students to do something that they could not have done without the technology.

In flipped classrooms, students watch 5- to 10-minute video lectures outside of class time. Rather than listening to an in-class lecture, students

> Project RED emphasizes that for the introduction of technology to be effective, instruction must also be meaningful.

instead spend class time working on, for example, math problems with the help of the teacher who is available to answer questions as students work through difficult material. Working through problems in class with the teacher at hand to help with difficult questions is particularly helpful to students who are learning material more advanced than their parents' abilities. If students were doing the problem sets at home, they wouldn't have the benefit of the teacher's help when they came across stumbling blocks. All told, these second-order changes allow for individualized instruction, which is what really leads to improved learning and improved results on tests. The benefit of teaching in a 21st century classroom is that you have technology to implement second-order changes that were not possible just a few years ago.

The authors of the Project RED study found that to maximize digital change effectively, nine steps had to be followed. I have listed six points here in order of statistical importance.

1. **Allowing access to technology in intervention periods for students.** Our students have grown up in a digital age whether or not they have access to technology in their homes. Virtually all are well versed in using technology. And yet, in many schools, students are asked to put away their devices and instead use paper and pencil.

2. **Monthly (or more) time for teacher learning and collaboration.** Admittedly many teachers much prefer to lead students in new learning rather than to learn new material themselves. Since there is so much to learn, however, it can only be done in collaboration with colleagues and on an ongoing basis. This learning time can partially overlap with Professional Learning Community time if the new technology can be used with lesson plans and assessment programs.

3. **On a daily basis, students collaborate online—be it for simulations, games, or projects.** Think for a moment how children learn how to use Twitter, Facebook, e-mail, the Wii, Xbox, or any online games. It all comes from trial and error and from collaborating with their friends.

4. **Technology is integrated into classes at least once a week.** As you will see in this book, deeper learning does not come just from using technology for technology's sake but rather from using technology to let students search for answers to problems just as they will have to do in any job that requires higher-level thinking skills.

5. **Weekly online formative assessments.** Good teachers know they have to constantly get feedback from students to know where to repair learning, when to re-teach, and when to move on and not to move on to new material.

6. **The lower the student-to-Internet-device ratio, the better the results.** This is especially important for lower-income students who do not have access to technology at home and who are falling farther behind those who do, in a world that increasingly demands Internet prowess. While it costs money to purchase digital devices, consider the devices of the industrial age. The Project RED study found that in a school of 1,500 students, $100,000 can be saved each year in paper and copier costs if they are replaced with digital devices. But one cannot forget the other costs of 20th century learning, such as individual desk printers and maintenance, filing cabinets, closets for notebooks, carts to push teacher supplies, desks with multiple drawers, bookshelves, scantrons for tests—the list goes on. All arising from dependence on paper. Of course the biggest saving comes from the time not used to print, staple, handout, collect, and re-handout. Digital work is instantly available and can be easily organized and found in a moment's notice (Greaves et al., 2010).

However, first-order change—like giving students computers—is not enough. The goal is to individualize learning. That does not mean that a teacher needs thirty different lesson plans—one for each student. Individualizing learning means implementing many of the second-order changes that are outlined in this book so that teachers can make sure each student has learned the material before moving on to the next section. Individual learning may even mean going beyond a traditional school year or having some students with fewer subjects than others.

As you read the following chapters, think how the six steps mentioned above can help change your classroom, school, or district little by little or all at once, remembering that you want to shoot for second-order integration of technology. Change is not easy for most people—students, teachers, and administrators alike—but the time and effort will be well worth it.

CLASSROOM EXAMPLES

As listed above, Project RED stipulates that second-order change calls for online collaboration. Consider online collaboration between students and teachers. Being able to return assessed assignments to students early is a positive change. If an assignment is due at 10:00 a.m. on Monday, the vigilant teacher can have graded many of the assignments before 10:00 a.m. if they were submitted by students online on Friday night, Saturday, or Sunday. If the class is self-paced, then students who enter class at 10:00 a.m. having already

(Continued)

Visit http://bit.ly/digitalclassroomteacherguide to access live links.

(Continued)

received their assessed work, can immediately ask for help on parts that were marked incorrect. So too, assignments submitted online on the deadline can be corrected by the teacher while students are working on projects or doing a class warm-up. I have found that improving the speed of return for my students means that they look at my comments more closely and then take more time to make improvements.

Another second-order change in my classroom is letting my students use multiple modalities in the classroom. For example, they might be typing on their laptops while at the same time watching a video lecture on their smartphones. In my class, smartphones are discouraged only if they are hidden, which usually means something mischievous is going on. The school where I teach is not on the high end in terms of income (27 percent free and reduced lunch). Furthermore, many of my students are English Speakers of Other Languages (ESOL), yet almost all of them come equipped with smartphones, iPods (which have full Internet access when connected to the school's Internet), or even tablets. I ask my students to write their homework assignments on their devices as I know they will not leave them at school, but they might forget to bring their homework planners home with them.

EDUCATOR CHALLENGES

Monday Morning Challenge: Discuss with your Professional Learning Community (PLC) examples of technology you have been using in your classroom. For each example, decide if it is a first- or second-order change. Select a first-order change and as a group decide how to make it a second-order one.

Tuesday Morning Challenge: In a department meeting, ask if anyone is having their students work on Internet-based assignments. Then debate whether the assignments mentioned are examples of first- or second-order change. If they have not reached the second tier, what might be done to reach this level?

Wednesday Morning Challenge: Create a QR code for a website you want your students to access with their smartphones or tablets. You might create, for example, a QR code that can be posted in the school hallway or on the school grounds that would lead students to a website with relevant information.

Thursday Morning Challenge: As a school, discuss the technology being used in your institution. Are you meeting the requirements of

FERPA, COPPA, and CIPA? If not, what changes can you implement to be in compliance? Take steps to ensure that all teachers are being responsible digital citizens.

Friday Morning Challenge: Use a search engine to find an innovative way to teach a content area you have been teaching for years. Since there are many resources online, you will be amazed at how many educators have put ideas and resources online that will be useful in your classroom.

2

Teacher Collaboration

Online Professional Learning Communities

- Learn about the numerous benefits of online PLCs
- Learn how to use several online tools to expand your PLC
- Learn several online tools for communicating with your PLC in real time

PROFESSIONAL LEARNING COMMUNITIES

This chapter will look at how teachers can use online resources to connect with other educators to expand their professional learning communities, acquire new curriculum content, learn about new pedagogical ideas, and collaborate with others. Being proactive about your own professional development will allow you to go beyond the often repeated ideas of your core peers and school district.

If you are going to learn to let your students pace themselves by their abilities, then you are going to be moving in a different direction from that of most of the teachers in your school who are accustomed to having all of their students in sync. This transition will be much easier if you begin to develop a network of colleagues beyond your school to help you explore questions and provide feedback. Learning networks are nothing new in schools. The names for these groups are varied; from Professional Learning Communities (PLCs) to Collaborative Learning Teams (CLTs) to Professional

> If you are going to learn to let your students pace themselves by their abilities, then you are going to be moving in a different direction from that of most of the teachers in your school who are accustomed to having all of their students in sync.

Learning Networks (PLNs). Since PLC is the most common term, that is the one that will be used throughout this book. PLC is defined here as a network of peers on whom a teacher can rely to explore new ideas and to offer feedback.

Your PLC does not have to be limited to the boundaries of your school or district. Teachers have long excelled at borrowing ideas from others to improve their teaching. The focus of this chapter will explain how to continue that practice via a network of people you may never meet but who can convey rich sources of methodology, feedback, and even virtual pats on the back when most needed.

Collaboration came to me by necessity. When I started teaching advanced placement (AP) classes, I was collaborating with a colleague who taught down the hall. When I later became an AP coordinator, my positive experience collaborating with my colleague led me to insist that teachers work in collaborative teams, even if it meant venturing outside of our school walls. Later when I was chosen a department chair, I asked teachers to download their lesson plan ideas to the school's shared network drive. Eight years later we are using our several networked folders to mine ideas from long-departed teachers and are regularly adding more ideas for generations to come. Currently, we are putting many of these ideas and lesson plans in the cloud for easier access. Not only do new teachers in our department have a place to go for lesson plan ideas, but over the years these lessons have been improved, innovated, and changed so many times that it is not fair to call a lesson the work of any one teacher. No one is completely reinventing the wheel, but rather improving the spokes and making the wheel move more efficiently. New teachers can breathe more easily because they have access to a series of lessons created by others in the school, allowing the new teacher more time to focus on learning the new material, figuring out what motivates their students, and determining how to improve class discipline.

EXPANDING YOUR PLCs TO SOCIAL MEDIA

PLCs were the brainchild of Richard DuFour when he was the principal of Stevenson High School outside of Chicago. He realized that getting educators to collaborate would stimulate better teaching through shared ideas. At my school we take advantage of our school-based PLCs to

- discuss lesson plans for upcoming units;
- differentiate between how to teach special education, English Speakers of Other Languages (ESOL), and mainstreamed students; and
- write and revise formative assessments and summative tools.

While PLCs might not always be as innovative as a "drive-by discussion" in the hallway for stimulating new ideas, they can be incredibly helpful to all teachers from newbies to veterans. But there are limitations to these school-based groups. Colleagues at a school site become so familiar with one another that they often settle into a predictable rhythm. Individuals learn what can be said and what cannot be said so as not to offend anyone. New members make changes and add new ideas, but the process needs to be continually changed—and that is unlikely to happen when your PLC is limited to the walls of your school.

Enter social media. The first thing I hear teachers say when I suggest following people on Twitter or looking at a blog is that they do not have time. Between grading, attending several weekly PLC meetings at school, and developing lesson plans, teachers often feel as if they are working the hours of first-year lawyers. Teachers need time to spend with their spouses and children and to enjoy some precious minutes of leisure. All of these things take time. Most people look at social media as a way to follow other people's lives and not as a way to improve their professional practice. But social media can be a very efficient way to gather new ideas and grow as an educator. Social media sites, such as Twitter, can add innovation and new ideas to school-based PLCs, as individual members learn online and then share new ideas at PLC content meetings.

> Social media can be a very efficient way to gather new ideas and grow as an educator.

USING TWITTER TO BUILD YOUR PLC

Not only is Twitter among the most used social media by your students, but it is an incredible resource for expanding a teacher's PLC. Started in 2006, the idea originated from the fact that cell phones were able to send 140 characters of information (spaces, periods, exclamations all count as characters) for a quick message. Twitter's popularity stems from its capacity to show posts to the whole world (unless you set the post on "Private"). Twitter now has a huge following among connected educators who use it to collaborate with others online, whom they may never meet in person. The service is so popular that approximately 243 million people use it each month (Smith, 2014). And Twitter is extremely easy to use! Teachers can use Twitter to

- learn exciting new ideas and quickly bypass the less important ones,
- click on web pages that offer in-depth ideas,
- speak with one or many teachers in a live or delayed fashion, and
- find valuable educators with whom to connect.

I check my Twitter feed (@kenhalla) two to three times a week. In a typical week I will use Twitter to click on many different web pages that will give me ideas on everything from content to pedagogy to new lesson plans. For example, during a quick check today I found posts including the following links:

- a way to chat online with US Secretary of Education Arne Duncan next week
- the best way to move desks around to create the ideal learning environment
- three simple ways to use smartphones in the classroom
- how digital writing is making kids perform better in the classroom

This all took me less than a minute. How often does one get to speak to the US secretary of education or even listen to a conversation with him and other educators? Perhaps you are a school leader looking for ideas for younger teachers. In a quick check of Twitter, you find several ways to help them that go beyond your own experiences. If the overall goal is to seek out ways to further individualize instruction for your students, you will need help from others far and near.

Getting Started on Twitter

- To join Twitter, go to twitter.com
- Go to the sign-up section on the right side of the page.

  - Fill in your name, e-mail, and password.
  - You will be taken to a new page, asking you several questions.
  - Answer the questions, push Submit, and you will now have your own account.
  - You will have your own Twitter name designated with the @ symbol and then the name you have chosen, such as "@kenhalla."
  - On this site and any others discussed in this book, if you check the "Remember me" box (as long as you are using the same browser and computer), the site will log you in automatically.

Tips on Composing Tweets

- To compose a Tweet, go to the Home tab on the upper right side of the page where you see a picture of a quill pen.
- Type your message in 140 characters or less. Press return. If your Tweet is too long, the exceeding characters will turn red.
- Good Tweets have links to web pages. Twitter will automatically shorten the web page addresses, known as URLs, to ten or fewer characters.
- Good Tweets might also include hashtags (#NGSS #STEM #Science), which you will learn about later in this chapter.
- You can address a Tweet to a particular person by using his or her Twitter handle @JohnDoe, or you can give credit to a group of people by including several Twitter handles: "Kudos to the organizers of this year's Science Fair @MrNelson, @MsGarcia." Your Tweet can share a useful link to an article, express your opinion about a current news event, or pose a question to everyone in your Twitter world. You could ask your online PLC "Does anyone have good resources for a lesson on poisonous frogs? #NGSS #STEM #Science"

---

kenhalla @kenhalla   5h
US Government Teachers Blog: Studying for the AP US Government
Exam usgovteducatorsblog.blogspot.com/2013/04/studyl...
Expand ← Reply 🗑 Delete ★ Favorite ••• More

Connecting With Other Educators

The key to using Twitter to expand your professional learning community is amassing as many new ideas and rich sources of information from other educators as possible ("How to Use Twitter to Grow Your PLN," 2012). Therefore, you will want to start following as many people as you can right away. To follow someone, tap on the "Follow" button at the top of his or her Twitter page. If you find that any one of the people you follow proves to be more of a nuisance than an asset, you can easily unfollow them. Once you start posting regularly, others may find your Tweets useful and start following you as well. There are several ways to find people to follow on Twitter.

- Use the search bar on the upper right side of the Twitter page to search terms that interest you. Any post that includes that word or phrase will pop up and you can begin following the people who Tweet about your topic of interest. Before you decide which people to follow, you can look at their Twitter descriptions and their recent posts to see if any of them would be a valuable asset to your PLC.

Visit http://bit.ly/digitalclassroomteacherguide to access live links.

- Find educators you admire on Twitter, and look at the people they follow (or who follow them). Then decide if you would also like to follow those people.
- Another way to expand your network is by scanning your message feed to see who your friends are retweeting. If you choose to retweet, proper etiquette dictates that you keep the originator's name in your message, somewhat in the same way you cite a source in a book.
- You can also find people by clicking on "#Discover" in the upper left for suggestions.

Search Google or other search engines for "educators to follow on Twitter" or be more specific and type "English teachers Twitter." Once you start amassing a group of people to follow, Twitter will start recommending like-minded individuals to you. This function of Twitter is a great resource to find others to grow your PLC. You will find that once you start following people and start posting relevant content (with URLs and hashtags), others will be likely to start following you. It's rather a reiterative process.

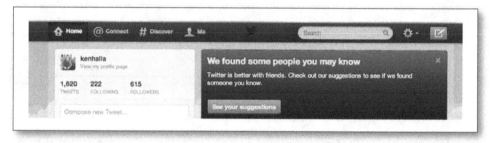

If you have time, go to a search engine and look for "Twitter4Teachers Wiki!" It is an amazing wiki listing of teachers at every level from elementary to high school, ESOL, special education, the arts and so much more. A wiki is a place where anyone can edit information, so you can go to the site and add Twitter names you find in your own research.

- Some people I follow who help all teachers, no matter the level or subject, are
  - Cool Cat Teacher = @letyijerina
  - We Are Teachers = @WeAreTeachers
  - Eric Sheninger = @E_Sheninger
  - Richard Byrne = @rmbyrne
  - Shelly Terrell = @ShellTerrell

If you want a friend or someone you are following to see your Tweet, simply add their Twitter handle (@Marisol) in the Tweet. After you learn about hashtags, you can add them to your Tweets so that people following the hashtag can easily find your Tweets. For example, I could Tweet "@ kenhalla #historyteacher #governmentteacher #economicsteacher #blogger." To see if people are including your Twitter handle in their Tweets, go to the "Notifications" tab on the top left of Twitter to see where you have been mentioned by others.

Using Storify to Save Tweets

Tweets remain on Twitter forever so if you want to view previous Tweets (your own or someone else's), you can simply scroll backwards through the Twitter feeds. But if you want to avoid scrolling through hundreds or even thousands of Tweets, you can use <u>Storify</u> to save the Tweets you find particularly helpful. As a matter of fact, you can save lots of digital sites on Storify. For example, you could save a video, a website, and a number of related Tweets from Twitter into one story to share with your students for a particular project. Since you can write long captions, you can use Storify to have your students write a report that seamlessly includes student writing, video clips that highlight the writing, Twitter comments, images, websites, and so on. Talk about a new way to put together information!

Go to Storify.com, create an account, and then on the top right go to "Create Story."

- Along the right side are a number of categories such as Twitter. In that case, just type in the name of person whose Tweets you want to clip and click enter. When the person's feed appears, simply drag the Tweet(s) to the left side.
- You can also tap on the URL symbol.

Visit http://bit.ly/digitalclassroomteacherguide to access live links.

- You can even add YouTube videos into your story.
- When you are done, be sure to save your work. You can edit it later.

For an excellent Storify tutorial and student example of a multimedia story, go to YouTube and search for "Storify Tutorial House Divided."

Using Hashtags to Have Conversations on Twitter

So far we have discussed static Tweets posted on Twitter. Sometimes, though, you might want to have a live conversation with other educators, your PLC, or even your students. Using hashtags is a useful way to keep all of the comments related to a particular conversation or topic in one place. To start a new conversation, create a unique hashtag, which consists of a string of characters preceded by the "#" symbol. Examples of some hashtags for your PLC might be #digitalclassroom101, #selfpacingstudents, #mathgames4u. You can also join conversations already in existence by finding hashtags created by others such as #STEM, #makerspace, #ushistoryclass. All you need to do is create a Tweet that includes the hashtag somewhere within the Tweet. If others are tweeting at the same time, you can have a multiperson discussion and watch the stream of comments appear just as you would with regular Tweets. It might sound crazy to have a conversation in 140 character bursts, but it is amazing how much can be discussed. Including URLs in your Tweets (along with the hashtag) is also a useful way to introduce outside sources of information to the conversation. Twitter conversations are a good way to encourage your more quiet students to participate in class discussion. Quiet students often find a voice on Twitter, which in turn inspires them with more confidence in the regular classroom. You can use hashtags to converse with teachers in your district, from around the country, or even from around the world.

To start a conversation using a hashtag:

> Quiet students often find a voice on Twitter, which in turn inspires them with more confidence in the regular classroom.

- Go to the Twitter search engine and type in your devised string of letters starting with the number sign #. For example #howtofindteachers. If no results pop up, then you know that no one else is using your hashtag.
- If someone else is using the hashtag you can still use it, but just realize that nonrelated posts might be streaming in. For example, "#chemistry" could involve conversations about science, college students taking a course, or a song named "chemistry."

- Then give the hashtag to your PLC members or your students with a time and date to start your discussion.
- If you do not want your many Twitter followers (yes, others will soon follow you on Twitter) to see this particular hashtag conversation, just precede your tweet with "@HideChat." When you use @HideChat, your Tweet will not be sent out to your followers' Twitter feeds. But your Tweet will be seen by anyone who searches for your hashtag.

- Below is part of a hashtag discussion between a colleague and me.

Utilize Twitter as Your Own Personal PLC by Searching for Popular Hashtags

- The website <u>Edudemic</u> is a site where both students and teachers can find hundreds of tips for integrating technology into the classroom. It has a list of <u>300+ Educational Hashtags</u> and an explanation of what each is about. This means you can converse live with others who teach the same level of content as you and enhance your classroom. If you really enjoy someone's ideas in a hashtag conversation, you can simply click on the name and start following that person, thus further building up your PLC.
- Finally, <u>Cybraryman</u> has hundreds of times and hashtags for teachers.
- If you cannot meet when the hashtag is having a live conversation, then you can simply search for the hashtag in the Twitter search box after the fact and scroll down the page looking for helpful comments and links.

The most popular hashtag for teachers is #edchat, which is used in weekly discussions. In fact, if you search the sites given above, you will find weekly discussions for any topic. Since the discussions are live, you will see comments from educators around the world popping up one after the other in short succession. To contribute to the conversation, just type in the hashtag somewhere in your Tweet and it, too, will appear. Here is just a small sampling of what you can find:

- #sschat   Social Studies Teachers   Mondays, 7 pm EST
- #musechat   Music Educators   Mondays, 8 pm EST
- #kinderchat   Kindergarten Teachers   Mondays, 9 pm EST
- #scichat   Science Teachers   Tuesdays, 9 pm EST
- #artsed   Art Educators   Thursdays, 7 pm EST
- #langchat   Language Teachers   Thursdays, 8 pm EST
- #elemchat   Elementary Teachers   Saturdays, 5 pm EST

Source: "How to Use Twitter to Grow Your PLN," 2012.

The hashtag #individualizelearning pertains specifically to this book. While in Twitter, type #individualizelearning into the search field to see what fellow readers are saying about how they are applying the resources in this book to their teaching practice. I will be checking the hashtag on a regular basis and would love to receive your insights and learn the ways that you are using this book to change your classroom.

USING GOOGLE+ AS A PLC RESOURCE

Another online PLC that has grown more quickly than Twitter or Facebook is Google Plus (g+).

Google+

- allows you to add (as opposed to link) videos,
- has two streams of information so you can take in items more quickly,
- has no limit on the number of words in a message,
- allows you to communicate either publicly or just to a select number of people,
- allows you to set up communities that can be made up of students or other teachers, and
- allows you to have video conferences with up to nine other people (Google Hangouts).

If you are signed into Google, then go to the top right of your screen and look for the icon of nine tiny boxes arrayed in a square. Click on the icon and a new screen will appear. Click on "g+." Alternatively just type in "plus.google.com" and then log in.

Visit http://bit.ly/digitalclassroomteacherguide to access live links.

Many people, like me, use both Twitter and g+ to find information to further their professional development. You will find that there is some overlap, as some people post the same information in Twitter and g+. I suggest checking out both and then deciding which you prefer. If you have never used either of them, I would suggest starting with only one until you have mastered it before trying to manage both at once.

- g+ is fairly intuitive to use. Look at the left side of the page. If you run your mouse over the "Home" icon you can very easily select what types of things you would like to do such as see your circles of friends, look at your photos, speak via a video "Hangout" with your friends, and more.

Google+ Communities

If you tap the "communities" tab, which is underneath the "Home" button, you can see all kinds of groups that Google thinks you might want to join. You can also start your own groups. g+ communities allow you to connect with like-minded people, but in a stream-like fashion as opposed to a live Twitter hashtag conversation. Explore g+ by using the search engine at the very top of the g+ page. To visit the pages, type in the terms below, much as you would do on Twitter when looking for new teaching ideas. Some sites you might want to follow are listed here.

- Google for Education is a site for teachers, maintained by Google.
- Edudemic is a great website filled with tips.
- Education Week is the definitive educational online resource for technology integration for teachers.
- Ken Halla is my Google+ feed.
- Education Revolution is where you can meet lots of other teachers.
- Google Certified Teachers is a site where teachers who have earned the highly selective "Google technology certified" endorsement put their posts, and you can join in as well.
- Google Apps for Education is another community for educators whose school systems have purchased the Google Drive suite for their teachers and students; it gives many insights into how to use the suite.

Following People on Google+

To add a person or group you want to follow, go to the search box at the top of the screen and enter in a name or a topic. When you find someone of interest, add him or her to your circles.

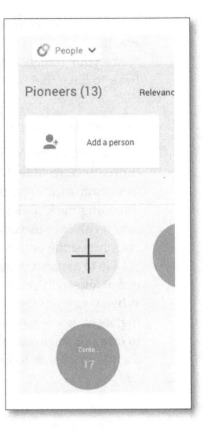

- To create a circle, look for the symbol with three circles on the left side of the screen and click on it.
- Then go to the tab that says "circles" and click on it.
- Next go to the "+" sign to create a new circle of people.
- Tap on the "add people" icon and type in their e-mail addresses (see picture below). You can then quickly add friends or create circles by clicking on names that are in g+
- The advantage of the circles is that you can create feeds that only some people can see and send these people messages. So, for example, you could create a feed for your students, and they could set it so you could not see all of their other messages.

Google+ Hangouts

We all know that meeting someone in person has benefits that cannot be matched by virtual meetings, but is it really necessary to conduct every meeting in person? The very best part of Google+ is its Hangout functionality. With Google Hangouts (GHO), you can initiate or participate in a video conference with up to nine other people. During these conferences, the person speaking will be the largest image on your screen, and you will also be able to see smaller images of the other participants—their facial expressions, hand gestures, emotions, and so on. Another great feature of GHO is that participants are able to share the contents of their desktops with the conference members (if you choose). One of the most amazing features of GHO is being able to have nine people all editing one Google Drive document (which you will learn about in Chapter 3) at once in real time while hearing each other talk, whether the participants are in different cities, states, or other countries. In this way, you could collaborate with teachers from several different areas to create, for example, a proposal for a conference explaining the various ways you all use student self-pacing strategies in the classroom.

Visit http://bit.ly/digitalclassroomteacherguide to access live links.

If your device (computer, laptop, tablet, phone) does not have a camera, then you can still be heard by the other participants and you can still share your screen and documents. Please note that all participants will have to have their own Google accounts.

Scheduling a Meeting Time

Before you can meet in a Google Hangout, you will need to decide on a mutually agreeable date and time for the meeting, just as you would with in-person meetings. If your meeting involves many people, rather than e-mailing back and forth several options and counteroptions, you might find it easier to use one of the many free Internet tools available to suggest and then settle on a meeting time.

Go to a search engine and look for a "simple meeting scheduler." A number of sites will show up. One of the simplest ones is called NeedToMeet. When you go to the website, you will be prompted for the title of the meeting, meeting notes (which is where you can put the time zone for the meeting in case you have attendees in different zones), and the duration. You can join the site or choose to use it without having a login or password. Hit "Select Times," and then select the days and times you want to set as options. Once you have selected the times, hit "Invite Attendees" and you will be given a URL, which you can send to the meeting participants (via e-mail, for example). Participants will then visit the site via the link, enter their names, and select the times they are able to meet within the given options. Once people submit their preferences, their choices can be seen by the other participants. This is usually a much more efficient way of selecting a mutually agreeable meeting time.

Starting a Google Hangout

- From Google.com, click on the nine-box icon > g+ > Home > Hangouts.

- Go the right side of the page and hit the "+" sign beside where it says "New Hangout" and then "Start a hangout."
- If you have previously e-mailed people from your Gmail account, their addresses should automatically pop up when you type in their names. If that doesn't happen, type in their Gmail addresses.
- Name the Hangout and then click on the video camera icon.
- To share your screen with people in the GHO, click on the green icon with the white arrow. When you place your cursor over the icon, you will see the words "screen share" appear.
- To share Google Drive documents, click on the Google Drive icon (the green, blue, and yellow triangle below).
- If other people share their desktops, just click on their video images at the bottom of the screen and whatever is being shared will dominate your screen. Otherwise, whoever is talking will be the image dominating your screen.

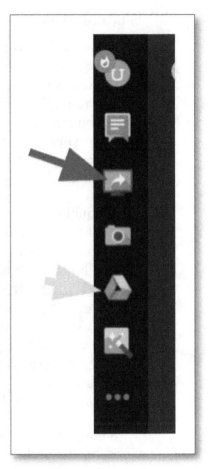

EXPAND YOUR PLC BY FOLLOWING BLOGGERS

Google+ and Twitter are ways you can get quick snapshots of information from other people. If you want to get more in-depth information, however, then you will want to look for some educational blogs to follow. Blog writers usually have a particular topic of focus that they want to share with others. Some of the most popular blogs include The Huffington Post; the celebrity gossip site TMZ; and 538.com, which uses statistics to look at many topics. Another way to think of blogs is as a series of short articles, known as posts, that the blogger puts online. You will find the bloggers' most recent posts on top. Readers can add their own comments below each post. Just as with Google+ and Twitter, a reader can interact with the writer as well as other readers about the blog post. Finding the right blogs can be a great way to improve your teaching craft by reading the ideas of others, learning what's going on in other classrooms, engaging with others in conversation, and contributing your own thoughts and questions to the conversation.

Visit http://bit.ly/digitalclassroomteacherguide to access live links.

Educator Blogs

Educators will want to find blogs that suit their styles of teaching. Some basic requirements might include having a visual or video, instructive comments about why an idea is useful in the classroom, and instructions on how to implement the suggested lesson in class. To find some useful blogs, you can start with the lists in this book or simply perform a Google search of your own. For example, if you are a math teacher, you might search for "high school math blogs," "high school math teacher blogs," or "math blog." There are several sites that house educator blogs, such as

- <u>Edublog</u>—a community of thousands of educational blogs broken into easy-to-find categories
- Edudemic's site has two useful blog sites
  - o <u>Edudemic's 50 Must See Blogs</u>
  - o <u>The Teacher's Guides to Technology and Learning/</u>
- <u>Free Tech 4 Teachers</u>—one of the most popular sites on the Internet for teachers. It offers four or five posts a day covering topics useful to every category of teachers.
- <u>English Teachers Blogs</u>
- <u>Math Blogs</u>
- <u>Top 50 Science Teacher Blogs</u>

A blog can be found for almost any aspect of teaching. Find blogs that work for you and that give you the kind of information that you need most. Some blogs simply discuss content while others offer tips on how to use technology. The four blogs that I author (<u>US Government Teachers' Blog</u>, <u>US History Teachers' Blog</u>, <u>World History Teachers' Blog</u>, and <u>Economics Teachers Blog</u>) offer both content and technology tips. Most blogs include a search engine, which is useful since older blogs can house thousands of posts. The search bar gives readers the option to quickly search for topics of interest, for example, "reading levels," "differentiation," "flipped classes."

> A blog can be found for almost any aspect of teaching.

BOOKMARKING IN THE CLOUD

By utilizing the resources of your several online PLCs, you will collect many, many web pages that you will want to save and revisit over and over again. A convenient way to save these sites is to bookmark them. Bookmarks are a way to save the URL and annotate it for later reference.

Some people save bookmarks on their laptop memory drive, but the problem with that is that you will be able to find those bookmarks only when you have access to that particular device. A better way to save bookmarks is by using a cloud-based tool so that you will be able to find your Internet pages on any device that is connected online.

Google Bookmarks

Chrome, Firefox, and Safari all have cloud-based bookmarks. However, keep in mind that using Google bookmarks is different from bookmarking in Google's browser, Chrome. If you set up your bookmarks in Chrome, you will be married to having Chrome on your Internet device, which might be a problem if you are using a device that does not have the Chrome browser.

To get started with Google bookmarks, type "<u>Google bookmarks</u>" into a search engine.

- Tap on the "Add bookmark" button on the left side of the page.
- You will be prompted create a label. Related sites can be added to the label later. In the example below, "News Sites" is the label, "New York Times" is the name of the bookmark, and www.nytimes.com is the URL. Once you are done, hit "Add bookmark."

You will eventually collect multiple labels for your various bookmarks. By hitting each of the titles on the left side of your page, you will be able to see just the websites under each label (for example, under the label News Sites, you might have bookmarks for The Economist, the Washington Post, and the Wall Street Journal). If you hit "Bookmarks," then you will be able to see all of your bookmarks. If you decide that you want to rename or delete a label, then tap on "Manage labels."

Visit http://bit.ly/digitalclassroomteacherguide to access live links.

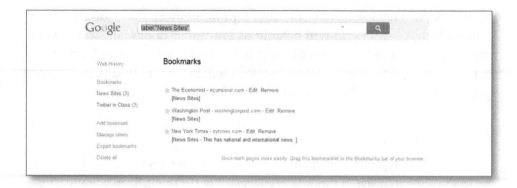

Saved.io Bookmarks

For alternatives to Google Bookmarks, conduct a search for "online book-marks." One of the simplest ones is Saved.io, which allows you to create bookmarks simply by writing "saved.io" prior to a URL. One drawback with Saved.io is that you cannot annotate your bookmarks.

- Go to the Saved.io site and sign up for an account. Once you are logged in, find a website you want to bookmark.
- Let's say it is the New York Times. Simply type "saved.io/" before the Times' URL as in "saved.io/nytimes.com," and it will be saved.
- If you want to have a category for your news sites, say "newspa-pers," you would simply add it before the URL as in "newspapers.saved.io/nytimes.com.

In no time, you will have multiple categories, also known as "lists" and plenty of links. Best of all, your bookmarks will be accessible on tablets, smartphones, and any computer.

Bookmarks allow for a notes' section where I often put login and password hints, such as "name of children's elementary school." It is not that I am worried that someone working for the bookmarking company will look at my personal sites. Rather it is a precaution in case the page was open on my computer and someone, unbeknownst to me, attempted to access one of my links. Instead of finding my actual login and password, they would see only the hint, which has significance to me alone. However, noting hints rather than actual passwords is not a foolproof security measure. Because the sites you visit will leave cookies on your computer, once you log in, you will be able to access the site without logging in again. Facebook is a good example of this. Once you log in, even after you turn off your computer and restart it, you will still be logged into Facebook. Banks and financial institutions are often an exception to this, insisting that you log in not only each time, but after only a few minutes of non-use. Thus, you should always use caution and never let a student or anyone you do not trust use your laptop.

SOME CLOSING THOUGHTS ON ONLINE PLCs

The key takeaway from this chapter is that you have endless options available to you when you utilize the web as a resource for expanding your professional development. The fact that information is available to you 24/7 whenever and wherever you have an Internet connection means that you can always be learning about new and innovative ways to help your students learn.

All of the sites mentioned in this chapter can be accessed on a laptop, smartphone, or tablet. For those of you who feel you do not have the extra time to look at Twitter feeds or to collaborate online, consider the time you spend waiting in line. While waiting in line or for public transportation, use your smartphone to briefly check Twitter for teaching ideas.

This chapter has taught you a number of ways you can access information quickly and how to save it for future use. It is my hope that this will help shake up your PLC meetings, if not help change your teaching in general. Once you have learned how to use the techniques in this chapter, you will revel in the discovery that you can acquire large gains in learning with minimal time investment.

Keep in mind that if you plan to move toward a more student-paced classroom, you will need lots of feedback from other educators who are traveling down the same road. You can start expanding that network by adding educators who use the hashtag #individualizelearning to your Twitter account. Expanding your network to those outside of your school

Visit http://bit.ly/digitalclassroomteacherguide to access live links.

will greatly enhance this effort. The sooner you set up your new professional learning network, the better. Following the educator challenges below might give you that jump start you've been looking for.

 At the end of each chapter, you will see the QR box below, which you can use on your smartphone to get to the links mentioned in this chapter. Alternatively, you can go to http://bit.ly/digitalclassroomteacherguide if you prefer to use your laptop.

CLASSROOM EXAMPLES

Once you have experimented with having hashtag conversations on Twitter with the members of your PLC, try starting a hashtag conversation with your students. For example, you could start an online conversation with your students on a day when school has been canceled (perhaps because of snow). In order to prevent students from falling too far behind due to the missed day of school, get them to share their ideas on the causes of the Civil War or conduct a character analysis of Odysseus. Use the hashtag #snowdaydiscussion (or something similar) to send out questions and respond to students' comments. Students are attached to their phones 24/7, so why not use this to your benefit? Once they get the hang of this, some students may even take the lead in conversations. Using this strategy, you could cover a normal lesson plan (such as the causes of global warming) over Twitter.

Housing all of your passwords in the cloud can save you in so many ways. For example, in the county where I teach, teachers need to remember many passwords. Several of my colleagues keep a paper notebook containing all of their passwords. But if the notebook is at school, and a teacher feels like calling in sick, he or she won't have the password on hand needed to request a substitute. On the other hand, anytime I need a county code, I simply access my cloud-based bookmarks. Remembering that you have to be logged into Google, know that no one else can see your comments for each bookmark, so it is perfectly feasible to put your login/passwords there. This also means that when you are teaching and need to get to one of your bookmarked sites, you can easily find it and spend more time with your students.

Twitter has helped me too many times to count. I learned the intricacies of Google Drive from posts on Twitter, I discovered Fakebook (see Chapter 5), and I even learned how to improve my techniques on Twitter—all from checking Twitter two or three times a week. Several of my friends unfailingly participate in hashtag discussions each week with other educators in their content areas. Even if they miss the conversation in real time, they can later search the hashtag to see what others said and thereby pick up new ideas for their classrooms. Twitter is also a rich source of many of my lesson plans.

On a weekly basis, I participate in a Google Hangout (GHO) with a group of people who are working on developing an educational app. We have team members in Russia, India, Germany, California, Arizona, Michigan, and Virginia. Many of us have never met in person, but that hasn't stopped us from collaborating and creating what we hope will be a game changer in education. On Google Hangouts, we can see and hear one another and can easily share both documents and our laptops and desktops. So, for example, I can show my fellow participants anything on my computer screen.

Other uses of GHOs might include

- meeting with your school PLC to discuss likely free response questions on the upcoming AP exam, collaborating with educators from a neighboring school district to improve test scores in your subject area; and
- working on a collaborative presentation with your colleagues.

EDUCATOR CHALLENGES

Monday Morning Challenge: Set up a Twitter account and find ten people to follow. Add five more each week to reach at least fifty people to follow during the next three months. During this period, commit to following the Tweets at least twice a week. Share (retweet) the interesting information you find with others.

Tuesday Morning Challenge: Post at least two Tweets per week on Twitter related to your field of expertise.

Wednesday Morning Challenge: Create a hashtag and use it to converse with other educators. Start small and try it out with a PLC in your school so you can sit in a room together and see how it works. Then branch out to other educators in a nearby school.

Thursday Morning Challenge: Start bookmarking the URLs in this chapter and in subsequent chapters using Google bookmarks. Then try to access the bookmarked items from another computer (in the library or on a friend's computer).

Friday Morning Challenge: Have everyone in your school PLC create a Gmail account. Then schedule a time to have a Google Hangout with them.

Twitter Hashtag Challenge: Use #individualizelearning to share the ways in which you are changing both your teaching and interactions with other educators. For example, you could post a Tweet sharing the URLs of the new websites you have discovered and include the hashtag #individualizelearning. Or you could post a Tweet including #individualizelearning asking other educators to share the sites they follow.

Visit http://bit.ly/digitalclassroomteacherguide to access live links.

3

Storing and Sharing in the Cloud

- Learn useful Google Drive techniques for the classroom
- Learn how to enhance and refine Google Drive documents
- Learn how to use Google Drive to improve the way you teach

The work you and your students create in the classroom can be placed online (in the cloud) using <u>Google Drive</u> so you can access it anytime or anywhere. This will allow you to collaborate more easily and get and give feedback in an efficient manner. Ultimately, it will also be a very useful tool for allowing students to be self-paced in your classroom.

One of the most used cloud-based software programs now in classrooms is Google Drive (formerly Google Docs). If your school purchased it, the suite is also known as Google Apps for Education. Google Drive is essentially a slightly simpler version of Microsoft's Office program. Since it is in the cloud, it is updated all the time and does not require any new purchases (i.e., you will continually have access to the latest updates for free).

Using the vernacular of Project RED as discussed in Chapter 1, Google Drive's use in the classroom can be either a first-order change or a second-order change. Since it has the full suite of documents, Presentations (similar to PowerPoints), spreadsheets, and so on, it can be a very convenient platform for students to turn in work. As with Microsoft, you and your students can also organize your work into folders. All of these are first-order changes that you can easily implement in your classroom.

But Google Drive also allows for second-order changes. You can have students working together from different classes or, for that matter, schools or even countries. You can use Google Drive to create formative assessment tests and quickly ascertain if a student should do some refreshment work on assignments. The list of potential second-order changes is limited only to you and your PLC's imagination. You can even use Google Drive to collaborate with other educators far from the doors of your school.

> The list of potential second-order changes is limited only to you and your PLC's imagination when using Google Drive. You can even use Google Drive to collaborate with other educators far from the doors of your school.

So let's go! The Google Drive suite allows you to create and store word documents, called Google Docs; Presentations (which is Google's word for PowerPoints); spreadsheets; questionnaires, called Forms; and drawings (which Microsoft calls Paint). You can also add a host of other items such as WeVideo, which allows you to virtually collaborate with others on what Microsoft would call Movie Maker.

Please note that Google Drive recently updated its look, and this book reflects that change. If you are looking at the older version, go to the round gear in the upper right hand side, hit "Settings," and then "Experience the New Drive."

GOOGLE DRIVE TECHNIQUES FOR THE CLASSROOM

Uploading

Google Drive allows users to upload files from other applications such as Microsoft (Word docs, Excel Spreadsheets, PowerPoints). If you use the free Google Drive associated with your Gmail, you will be given 15 gigabytes of space. How big is this? I have all my files for ten classes, all of my personal data, and even the manuscript of this book and have used only 12 percent of my total allotted space. This is because anything started from scratch in Google Drive does not count against your total space allotment. Since you can upload an entire course folder in just a few minutes, it will not take much time to put everything you need in the cloud. Then you will be able to access all of your work from your smartphone, tablet, or any computer in the world. No longer will you need to drag your computer home with you, keep track of several flash drives, or worry about something important being left behind on your desktop.

- To upload a file or folder, go to the down arrow on the upper left side of Google Drive and look for the "New" button. Once you tap on it, you will see "File upload" and "Folder upload." Then you will need to find the item on your laptop that you want to upload.
- Once you have found it, click on it and push upload. You may want to convert your Microsoft documents to Google ones, in which case you have to go to the gear symbol at the top right.
- A new screen will appear, and you can click on the option you want, such as one that allows you to convert.

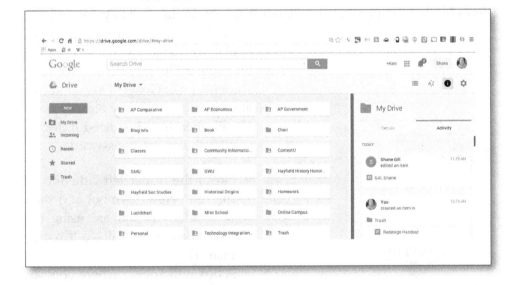

Google Drive Folders

You can use Google Drive Folders to have students submit completed assignments online as soon as they are done rather than have students wait to hand them to you in class. As with any new endeavor, there will be some adjustment phobia. But very quickly your students will prefer the online method for turning in work. There are several time-saving benefits to submitting work online for both you and your students. You and their parents will appreciate students' newfound organization. Using the search bar in their Google Drive accounts, students can find anything instantaneously. Students can easily share work with their peers without having to make copies. You will no longer have to waste time handing back work and instead can concentrate on grading in real time. If an assignment is due Tuesday at 10:00 a.m., I try to start grading early Tuesday morning or on Monday night so that most of the students have their graded work returned to them before it is officially due. If I add comments to a student's file in Google Drive, the program will let the student know by showing the title of the file in bold font. This is how my students know that their work has been graded. Since my students have come to expect my quick grading turnarounds, when they enter class at 10:00 a.m., some will ask why their work has not yet been graded. You may not want to put yourself under that kind of pressure, but you will come to appreciate your students' seeking out quick feedback, facilitating their ability to improve their work almost in real time.

The first thing you will want your students to do is to create a folder for your class on their devices. Folders are no different from the ones your students have in their backpacks, except these are digital. Just as your students

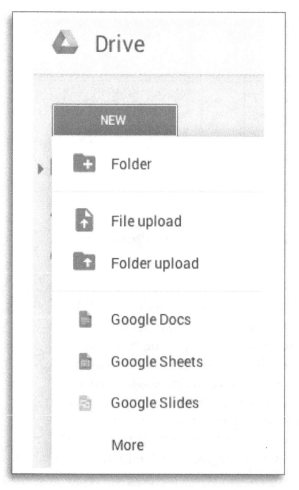

have folders or interactive notebooks, you are going to help them do the same in Google Drive. Have your students go to Google Drive and create an account. If they already have Gmail, then they just need to log in in with their Gmail password.

- Go to the upper left side and to the red "New" symbol and then to "folder." If you are using the older version, you will see "Create" instead.
- A box will appear where you can give the folder a title. I would suggest having the students label the folder with the name of your course so that everyone has, for example, "Biology 101" in their Google Drive.
- Then have the students click on the folder so it turns red. Then go to the "New" button and to "folder" and create a subfolder that is named for the first unit you are covering in your course.

Google Drive Documents

Now let's go to a simple document. You are going to create your first document or instruct your students in doing the same.

- To begin, click on the folder where you want it to go to so it turns red. Then go to "Create," and then go to "Document" and click on it. In the middle of your screen, a document will appear looking every bit the same as what you are used to in Microsoft's Word program, but now you are in the cloud.
- If you forget to click on the appropriate folder, then just right click on the assignment, go to "Move," and then navigate to the correct folder.
- Next, when you open up a document, it will ask for a title. I always tell my students to name it first with the number for the period of the class they are taking with me, then a space, their name, a space, and finally the name of the assignment we are working on in class. For example, "2 Halla Questions on Homer." If you are an elementary teacher, you might have the date go before your name. When files are labeled in this manner, a teacher is able to see the documents students have shared in an organized fashion, making it much easier to enter into a grade book.

- Now run your cursor over the icons starting on the left at the top of the page (see image above). The first symbol will say "Print" and the second, "Undo," and so on.
- An icon with which you may be unfamiliar is the hyperlink symbol, which looks like a link from a chain. Click on the hyperlink icon when you want to insert a hyperlink (URL) from a web page onto an image or word. To do this, go to the web page, drag your cursor over the URL, and then hit the "Control" and "C" buttons (that is the copy command). Then go back to the hyperlink symbol on your document page and press "Control" and "V" (that is the paste command) on your keyboard, and it will be pasted into the space.
- You can also instantly undo something by clicking forward or backwards on the arrows ↶ ↷.

Visit http://bit.ly/digitalclassroomteacherguide to access live links.

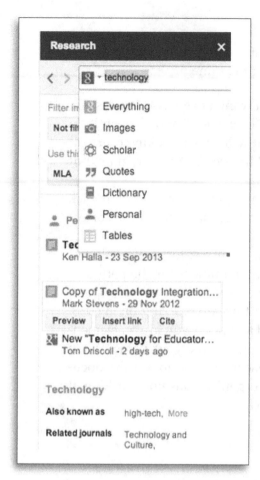

Everything else on that line will be familiar to you from the type of text you want, to whether you want to bold letters, or underline them, center them, and so on. One change from a Word document is that if you want to have a font size that is not normal, such as 9.5, just click on the font number, delete what is there, and type it in.

Another great feature of Google Drive documents can be found under "Tools" > "Research." You will see a pop-up window on the right side of the page where you can then input your topic into the research window. If you hover your mouse over the topic, you can choose to preview, insert a link in your document, or even add a citation at the foot of the page. Underneath your research window, you can choose the style of citation you need (MLA, APA, or Chicago). When you click on the research window, you can choose to search specifically for images, dictionary, scholar, and more.

Using the Cloud to Stem Plagiarism

Unfortunately some students will not be able to resist the temptation to plagiarize from Internet sources and copy from peers since it is so easy. Therefore, you need to be proactive and thwart plagiarism and copying early on. The best way to do this is to educate students about proper digital citizenship by showing them how to cite sources correctly. It is also important to let students know that you will be investigating suspicious passages from their work. They should quickly get the message that they won't be able to get away with not citing their sources.

> Unfortunately some students will not be able to resist the temptation to plagiarize from Internet sources and copy from peers since it is so easy. Therefore, you need to be proactive and thwart plagiarism and copying early on.

- If you see a series of words that are too good to be true, copy and paste them into a search engine. If the student copied the passage, the source will appear in your search.

- Once your students have all turned in their work, you can put a questionable (as in possibly copied) stem in the Google Drive search engine at the top of the page. If any other student's work includes the same line, that file will appear.
- If you are working on the assignment with other teachers, send them the same string of words and have them also use their class folder's Google Drive search engine where it says "Search Drive." Usually if you catch students doing this early, they will be freaked out and be less like to plagiarize later.
- You can also go to "File" and then "Revision History" and click on earlier versions of the document. The earlier versions will list the time that it was created and if there is only one, you can assume it was either uploaded (something I discourage in my class) or copied and pasted. Usually the students make some mistake such as pasting in one version with the other student's name. Since you can see all the changes, all you need to say is "I see you deleted "Joey's name at 1:13 a.m." Of course, administering assessments on a regular basis will tell you who is doing the work. You can also use "Revision History" to look at your own earlier versions of a document in case you would like to return to a previous version or see the changes your colleague made on a document you are collaborating on.

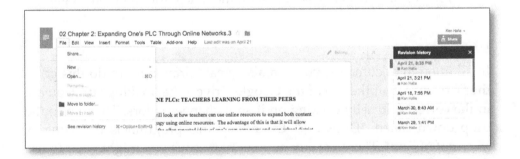

REFINING GOOGLE DRIVE DOCUMENTS

Inserting Images

Inserting images into documents adds a nice touch. It is my belief that having an image at the top of an assignment adds another important dimension to it. Since many of us think in images, seeing one at the top of an assignment will better connect the information for students in their memories.

Visit http://bit.ly/digitalclassroomteacherguide to access live links.

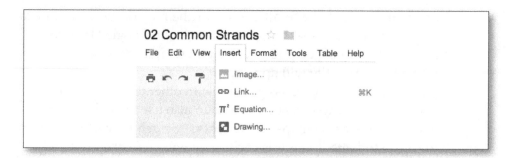

- To insert an image, go to the page and hit "Insert" and then "Image."
- If you click on the first symbol for adding an image, it will bring up a new window where you can search for a saved image. Additionally, any time you run your cursor over an item, a description of it will pop up.
- But since you are in the cloud, you could also click on "By URL" and add in a URL from a web image. This will save you the time of downloading and uploading the image. To get the image URL, just right click on the picture and it will say "save image address" or "save image URL."
- You can use EasyBib (see Chapter 1) to create citations for images. There are also sites such as <u>Creative Commons</u> (Google it!) that allow you to use their images without having to receive permission for items that might be made public, provided you follow the guidelines of the site (such as not using the image for commercial gain).

Drawing

In addition to documents, you can also create drawings. To do this go to the "Create" tab at the top of the Google Drive suite, making sure you are in the correct folder by clicking on it so it changes colors. Then go to the drop down called "Drawing." Essentially this program is the same as Microsoft's Paint. There are any number of reasons you might want to use this. You or your students could diagram a sentence. You could upload a map ("Insert" > "image") into a document and then label the map or label parts of a flower for biology.

- As with most of the other applications in this chapter, go to the "Insert" button, then "Line" and you will see the "Scribble" button, which is the one you will want to use most often. Click on it and start dragging your cursor about your image.
- Once you are done scribbling, click on the pencil image ![pencil icon] , which won't appear until you draw your first line. Clicking on the

pencil image will allow you to change the color of the line. To alter the width of the line, click on the icon with three lines as seen above. By going to "Insert" and "Line," you can get a line that you can draw from one item to another. Whatever key you want to use, just hover your mouse over it, and a word will pop up telling what it is used for. The best way to learn at this point is just to try and to make mistakes.

- You can write on your image by clicking on the text box 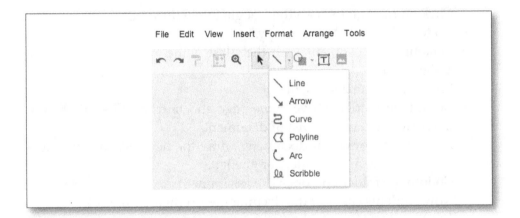 , dragging out a corner, and writing inside the box.

- From inside a document, you can create a drawing by going to "Insert" and then "Drawing." When you are done, press "Save and Close" and the drawing will be inserted into the document.

Sharing Google Drive Files With Students and Colleagues

There are many great advantages to using Google Drive. Perhaps the greatest one is that all changes are saved instantly. Secondly, you can share your files, collectively or on a case-by-case basis, with up to ninety-nine others who can collaborate instantly. The first time your students collaborate they will find it odd to see other students' cursors (their names will appear beside them) inside their document, but they will soon learn to maneuver around these. If you have worked collaboratively via e-mail in the past, consider how many times you or your students have e-mailed a document back and forth to each other until it is complete. With Google Drive, you need never do this again. Now you can insert comments ("Insert" > "Comment") or even just make corrections that collaborators can view through Revision History without ever having to e-mail anything.

Visit http://bit.ly/digitalclassroomteacherguide to access live links.

Perhaps the greatest advantage of working in the cloud is that all changes are saved instantly. Secondly, you can share your files, collectively or on a case-by-case basis, with up to ninety-nine others who can collaborate instantly.

There are two primary ways you can share documents with colleagues and students. For example, you might want to share with your students a document that contains instructions for an assignment. You can give students the URL for the Google Drive document by pasting the URL into a platform such as Blackboard or Moodle.

Then instruct students to take the following steps.

- Click on the link to open the Google Drive document.
- Go to "File" and "Make a copy."
- Rename the document with their last name and the name of the assignment.
- Close out of the document.
- Go to their Google Drive home page and find the "Recent" link at the bottom left of their list of documents.
- From the list of recent documents, drag the new assignment document into one of the folders on the left.
- Go into the folder and open the assignment.
- Now students can edit the document with their own work.
- To share the work with you (or their fellow students), go to the upper right side to the blue "Share" button. Click on the share button and type in the teacher's or the student's Google e-mail address.
- There are levels of sharing (Can Edit, Can Comment, and Can View). Have the students select the appropriate level of sharing for each given situation. Generally the teacher wants to have the student set it for "Can Edit."

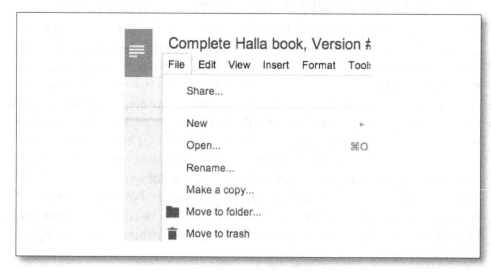

- On the lower left side of your Google Drive home page, you will see a folder called "Incoming." Those of you using the older Google Drive version will see "Shared." Click on this, and you will see all the documents that people have shared with you.
- If you use my naming format, the files will be organized by class and ready for you to grade.

This is a suggested procedure for grading student assignments.

- In the older version of Google Drive, you will see a blank check box. Once you have clicked on each corrected assignment, right click on one of them and all will be removed. In the newer version of Google Drive, you will just have to right click on each item and press "remove" as you finish each item.
- The files are no longer in your Google Drive account, but your students will still see that they have shared the item with you. They can go to their "Share" button and look at who has access to the item. So if you want to have your students re-submit something after you have taken it out of your "Incoming" folder, have them go to the "Share" button and click on the "X" beside your name, which will delete it. After that they can resubmit your name to be shared and it will reappear in your "Incoming" folder.
- If you would rather keep the assignments after you have commented on them, I suggest that you create a folder for each assignment.
- Go to "Create" > "Folder" > (name the folder) > "Create."
- The same principle then applies. If you check the box after commenting on each file, you can then move the checked files all at once into another folder, in this case the folder specified for that particular assignment. Right click on one of the checked files, select "Move to" > select the correct folder > "Move."
- If a student has made corrections on his or her assignment based on your feedback, the name of the file will be bolded, letting you know that it is time for you to look at the work again.
- Once you have made corrections on a student's work, right click on the line in your incoming list and then hit the "Remove" button.

Another use for a Google Drive document is to have your students share their first draft of a paper with you or with fellow students for feedback. Once the draft has been shared, those individuals may comment on the document

- The comment icon looks like a speech bubble . When you click on the comment button, a side screen will appear on the right side of the page that will allow you to insert comments.
- Alternatively you can go to the "Insert" tab and then to "comment." Now your students can see your comments on each section that needs work. If you are teaching a writing class, you can live edit student papers with having to walk around the room. This might be a difficult concept to grasp at first, but remember that any file in Google Drive is simply a web page. So when you and your student share a file, you are both in the same document. Students can rework the draft, click on your comment, press "resolve" and the comment will then be deleted. Since it is a web page, you also will never need to carry a flash drive around as all you need is an Internet connection and a browser.

BEYOND DOCUMENTS

Splitting Your Screen

If you want to grade assignments and immediately put them in your gradebook, then you will want to split your screen. On many computers all you need to do is to open up two Internet windows (or one browser window and one Google Drive document).

- Go to the bottom of the screen, right click and press on the line that says "vertically split your screen."
- Now go to the bottom of your screen and right click on your mouse pad and hit the part of the screen that says split vertically or horizontally.
- If you want to change the size of each half so that one has one-third and the other has two-thirds, then put your cursor on the edge of one side until an arrow appears and then draw the side to make it larger or smaller. On an Apple laptop, this is the only way to split a screen short of purchasing an online app to do so.

Presentations

The next item under documents is "Presentation." I sometimes use several slides at a time for when I flip my classes (see Chapter 5). What I love about these presentation slides is that I can give my students the URL for each presentation and, if I later edit the slides, I do not have to give them an updated version or a different URL since the original URL will lead to the updated version. Best of all, one can include video from YouTube very easily within the presentation slides. If you do share YouTube videos with your students, make sure you include proper citations and get permission if you are making the Presentation public.

When I started using Google Drive, I first uploaded all of my PowerPoints. Working on the PowerPoints within Google Drive is incredibly easy.

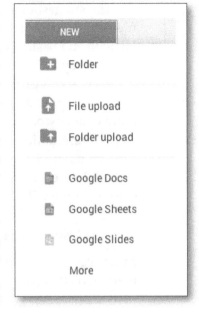

- To upload a Microsoft PowerPoint (or any other item), go to the upper left and tap on the word "New" and then "File upload or "Folder upload."
- If you are starting from scratch, when you first open the Presentation file, you will be prompted to select a background.
- Go to the "Insert" tab on the upper left side. You will see a text box for inserting lettering.
- You can also insert word art, a table, an image, lines, shapes, animations, and more. You will want to remind your students to properly cite whatever they use and to get appropriate permissions for anything they make public.
- If you want to insert a video, click on "Video" and you will be taken to a YouTube search engine. Write the title in the box, press "Enter," and your video will appear. Double click on it, and it will be added to your Presentation. If you put your cursor on the end, you can stretch or shrink the image.
- To insert new slides in a Presentation, click on the "Slide" menu option next to "Insert." You will be able to choose which type of slide you would like to insert.

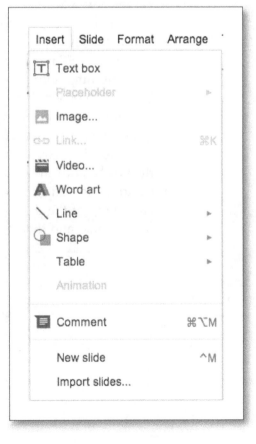

The suggestions offered in this chapter are a good way to start implementing second-order change in your classroom. Once you become familiar with the basics, you will find that there is a lot more you can do that extends beyond the tools listed in this book.

As you can probably tell, my style of teaching is hands on rather than straight lecture, as I believe that students learn more by muddying their hands than by passively listening. The best way to create and view Google Drive Presentations is on a laptop or desktop computer. Although you can see most of the applications on a smartphone or tablet, you cannot manipulate everything as you can on the laptop. But, in a year or so, Google Drive will likely be upgraded so that use on tablets will be easier.

How to Use Google Forms

Every year I have to collect student and parent e-mail addresses for our gradebooks. I used to pass around a sheet of paper and then struggle trying to decipher everyone's handwriting. Other times, we want to collect answers from students after they have watched a video. Now, I accomplish these tasks easily and painlessly by using Google Forms.

- Go to New > More > Google Forms.
- You will be prompted to enter a file title and to select a background.
- You will then be prompted to enter your first question. I always start with the LAST name (which I emphasize with capitals to catch my students' attention).
- Beside "Question Type," you would click on "Text" in this case—although there are many other options. Depending on the type of question you choose, your screen will change.
- Then decide if you want to make it a required response by checking the box beside "Required" or "Optional."
- Continue to add questions until you are done.
- At the top of the page look for the words "View Live Form." Click on that link, and then copy the URL and send it to your students.

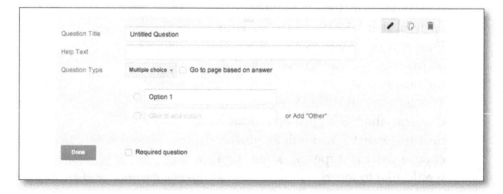

Look at the image below, which illustrates a completed quiz. Very quickly you can eyeball it to see if your pupils put down all of the correct answers. This is a very useful form to create when you want to collect information from students at the beginning of the year. I use it as a quick way to get parent e-mails, phone numbers, and so forth.

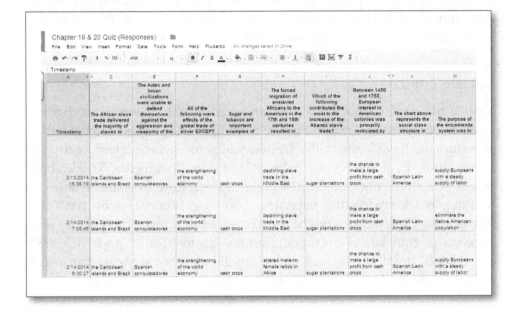

Templates

Instead of creating your own Google Forms from scratch, as a beginner, you might want to search for forms that have been created by others. There

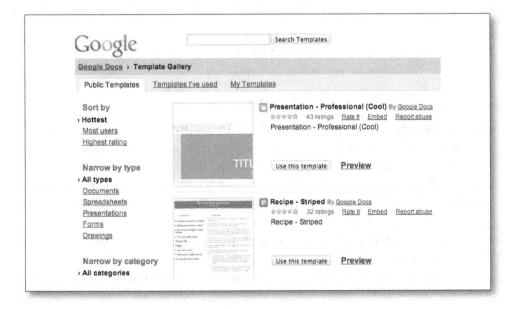

Visit http://bit.ly/digitalclassroomteacherguide to access live links.

are many, many templates for documents, Presentations, forms, drawings, and spreadsheets. To find them, go to a search engine and type "Google docs templates" (see image above). When you find a template you want to use, simply hit the "Use this template" button and it will open that particular Google Drive application. You will then be able to start editing the template to fit your particular needs. Once you have finished editing, go into your Google Drive account and click on "Recent" on the lower left, and you will see the new template saved.

Google Translate

One of the classes I teach is a mainstreamed World History class that has been combined with English Speakers of Other Languages. Almost half of the students have been in the United States for two or fewer years. For those students, it sometimes helps to translate documents. Think about when you are trying to help a student to learn how to write. The key is writing, not knowing the language. Likewise, students who have just come to the United States might want to see a full translation of your entire project. To translate a document, simply go to "Tools" and "Translate document." It will not be perfect, but it will help your students immeasurably. You can find even more languages by going to Google Translate.

Math Symbols

If you look closely at the symbols at the top of a Google Drive document, you will notice no math symbols. But you can pop them in very quickly by going to "Insert" and then to "Equation." Now you can add equations very easily.

Adding Applications to Your Google Drive Account

Another wonderful advantage of Google Drive is that you can add apps to it. For example, WeVideo is a cloud-based app that several people can work on simultaneously to create a video. WeVideo allows you to mix video with pictures, sounds, graphics, and words. The great thing about WeVideo is that it is compatible with both Microsoft-based computers as well as Apple devices.

There are plenty of other apps that you can add to your Google Drive by clicking on "New" > "More" and then looking for apps that you think might be helpful to you in your classroom. For most apps, you should be able to find tutorials on YouTube that will help you get started with the basics.

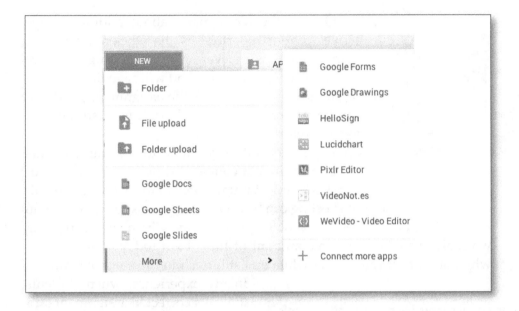

Syncing Google Drive With Your Laptop

When people start using the cloud, many worry that their files are not safe. Even though everyone who accesses the Internet from a computer is susceptible to viruses that could destroy all of their documents, most people still want their work saved on their laptops. If this is a concern of yours, you can choose to sync your Google Drive files with your computer or computers. If Google Drive is synced, any work edited in the cloud version of Google Drive will also show on your computer and any work done on your computer (on those synced files) will also appear on Google Drive.

- To sync your cloud version of Google Drive to a saved document on your laptop, go to the top right side of your Google Drive main page and tap on the round gear symbol, which is your settings tab.
- You will then see "Download Google Drive." Go to the downloaded program, click on it, and let it run the program.
- Go to the round gear on the upper right side of your folder page, tap it and "Settings" > "General" > "Offline," and check the box to start syncing with your laptop.
- It will differ depending on your computer, but somewhere on the desktop you will see the Google Drive icon. Clicking on it will allow you to see your files.

Visit http://bit.ly/digitalclassroomteacherguide to access live links.

- Now each time you update documents on the cloud, as soon as you open up your "base" laptop, it will sync with what is online.

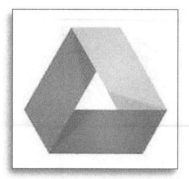

One of the nicest parts about adding Google Drive to your repertoire is the efficiency you will gain. Grading will never again mean dragging folders home, or losing items. You will save time by adding in grades as you mark the assignments, and you can have more time to work with your students or even to relax!

An important ingredient to having students moving through a course at different paces is grading work almost immediately. This is not as difficult as it may seem. Some correcting can be done during class so students who need help can see teacher feedback right away. Given that correcting work always takes the same amount of time, be it today or next week, why not mark it right away while it is still fresh in the students' minds?

> An important ingredient to having students moving through a course at different paces is grading work almost immediately.

In my experience, when students look at a corrected assignment on a paper, they are less likely to look at comments in that medium than on a digital copy such as a Google Drive document. Students, like most of us, also appreciate timely feedback when the assignment is still uppermost in their minds. Giving comments a few weeks after work has been turned in often means a student will be less inclined to closely study the corrections needed.

Here is the QR code for the links in this chapter. Alternatively, you can go to http://bit.ly/digitalclassroom teacherguide

---

CLASSROOM EXAMPLES

My students have all of their work in files that look like real notebooks, only digitized. This first-order change allows them access to their work at all times. No more worries about forgetting work when they move from friend to friend or even parent to parent. Since work can be instantly shared with me, there is also no forgotten homework. This means that students can also instantaneously see my corrections on their assignments and work with me or peers to improve work.

We also use Google Drive documents to work in small groups; but, unlike traditional classes, we are not limited to just those in the classroom at the moment. If it is appropriate, we share the folders with students in other classes. For example, one year, after the advanced placement exam, a colleague and I combined our AP US history and AP US government students into a very large classroom and had juniors and seniors collaborating across grade levels and with students not even in their same class schedule. Similarly we have also worked with students from other schools.

What about when your students are writing? Perhaps you know a page that can help them on the Internet to better learn a concept. Simply insert the link in your comments and your students will quickly be able to go to your recommended page. Likewise, if you keep a page with all of your assignments on it and links to them, if a new student comes in midyear, you can make a copy of the document, amend it, and in short order have all of the assignments for the new student easily accessible. The key is thinking that differentiating is okay and that separate pacing may be necessary for the special education, ESOL, or any other students with unusual situations. If you think about it, using cloud-based assignments will allow you to let students work at their own pace and for you to mingle more with each of the students as you explain and re-explain each of the concepts. In my school, we have a built in remediation period every other day. But because of the self-pacing my students are already doing, there is no need for the remediation period since it is being done every class period with the students who need it and there is no need to wait for a designated time.

In my department, members of the PLC share their folders with one another and with the administration. No longer do we need to e-mail our administrator our PLC notes. Instead she just goes in our shared PLC folder and looks at our work. Likewise, we share our entire class assignments instantly with other PLC members or even teachers in other schools. This allows for instant collaboration among teachers. Since Google bolds any document that another person has worked on, when you open your folder, you instantly know if someone else has made a change.

EDUCATOR CHALLENGES

Monday Morning Challenge: Commit to uploading a complete folder of one of your classes into Google Drive. Once you have done this, promise yourself that you will use only Google Drive for the entire year for one class. Understand that it will take time to adjust, but the commitment now will mean you will gain efficiency, and in a year you will gladly be putting all of your work in the cloud.

Tuesday Morning Challenge: Have your students create a folder for your class and put all of their work into it on a daily basis. Realize that some students will need additional help over a period of weeks, but commit to the challenge and student productivity will greatly improve.

Wednesday Morning Challenge: Give your students a short research assignment and have them use the Google Drive document research tool to find and cite information. Have them turn in the assignment with five or six citations.

Thursday Morning Challenge: Collect student information such as home phone numbers and parent e-mails using a Google Drive form. Now when you need to contact parents, you can access it no matter where you are.

Friday Morning Challenge: Try collaborating with other teachers on creating a common PLC assignment. Think of a project you might want to create, share it with the other members on your team, and have each of you make additions. Remember, you can insert comments in the margin to give one another a heads-up as to what you are thinking. You might even raise the bar and collaborate with members of another school's PLC using a Google Hangout and the document. This would be a second-order change, as you could create an assignment in real time with educators you would be left to e-mail with at best.

Twitter Hashtag Challenge: Use #individualizelearning to Tweet ways you are using Google Drive in your classroom. You could share a lesson plan that you have developed on Google Drive by pasting the link to the file in a Tweet (including the #pacingdigitallearner hashtag) to ask others for ideas on how you might improve the lesson.

Part II

The Self-Paced Student

4

The Self-Paced Anchor

Flipping the Classroom

- Describe a flipped classroom
- Explore online tools for flipping
- Learn about flipping leaders you can access online

Flipping the classroom has been growing in popularity. Flipping can be narrowly defined as posting lectures online and following up with an interactive in-class assignment. Flipping can also be a tool for second-order change that will allow teachers time to provide more individualized instruction in and out of the classroom. This chapter will tell you how to use the resources you learned about in the previous chapters to flip your own classrooms.

A number of years ago one of my administrators commented that I liked to lecture. Actually the Socratic Method was my instrument of choice to teach my students, but the comment stung, as there were definitely too many teacher-led lectures in my classroom. There was some comfort in lectures; after all, they had worked for me as a student, so surely it was an effective way to teach, right? But the moment of truth came in 2007 when my students were assigned to create a blog post that had to have images, several embedded videos, and answers to a number of questions on the causes of the Civil War. They worked while I paraded around the computer lab checking on their progress. After the work was done, I asked a number of questions to see if they had learned much. Once they understood the material, they were given a quiz, knowing that they could use anything on their blogs to answer my questions. To my utter amazement most passed with flying colors. Wait, you say, anyone could do that given that they had their work right in front of them. But the students had found the answers, synthesized the research, and now could answer in-depth questions and then do well on both an open-blog quiz and a closed-book standardized test a few weeks later. Something was up! Having the students interact with the material using the Internet resulted in a revelation for me—they were learning more effectively and retaining knowledge better.

> Having the students interact with the material using the Internet resulted in a revelation for me—they were learning more effectively and retaining knowledge better.

WHAT IS FLIPPING?

A flipped class can begin with a video that is designed to boil the most important parts of a traditional lecture into one succinct screencast that can be watched over and over again by students. The video should be ten minutes or less. Considering that a student will probably take notes and have to stop the video, a ten-minute clip can easily take twice as long for students to go through. Students who need more time are able to watch the video again and again while students who catch on quickly can move on at a faster pace, effectively individualizing the class. After watching the video at home, students can then enter the classroom and begin working on group projects or problem sets, having already been exposed to the key points of the material. This format gives the teacher more time to interact on a one-to-one basis with students.

As you read through this chapter, think of the definition above and know that I will be using terms such as "flipped video" to discuss the screencast that students watch on their own time and a "flipped class" to discuss what goes on at the school.

As with most technological uses in the classroom, flipping is fairly new. Most believe it harkens back to Maureen Lage, Glenn Platt, and Michael Treglia of the University of Miami who published the paper "Inverting the Classroom: A Gateway to Creating an Inclusive Learning Environment" (Lage et al., 2000) The professors were teaching an introduction to economics course and found that their students preferred seeing video at home and different types of hands-on learning in the classroom.

Another professor some studies credit with early flipping is Eric Mazur of Harvard who claims to have been flipping for twenty-two years.

Mazur hits the nail on the head in attacking traditional teaching when he says, "Simply transmitting information should not be the focus of teaching; helping students to assimilate that information should" (Berrett, 2012). Essentially this is why lectures should be limited to ten minutes. If you are speaking for much longer, the students are not learning by doing, which is always the most effective way to retain information. Instead they will be passively listening with no way for you to know they have effectively received the information. Mazur admits that not all of his students or colleagues like flipped videos since it takes time to make the change to an inverted environment (Berrett, 2012).

High school teachers often credit Jonathan Bergmann and Aaron Sams for coming up with the flipping idea. In 2007 Bergmann and Sams were high school science

> Learning by doing is always the most effective way to retain information.

teachers who were looking for a time-saving device. Having acquired the technology to record lectures, they did just that (Noonoo, 2012). The time was right, and the idea started to catch on (Bergmann & Sams, 2012). But it wasn't until Sal Khan came along that it really caught fire with educators around the United States. Khan wanted to help his niece learn math and since they lived apart from each other, he started to put math videos on YouTube and quickly noticed that others were using them. Khan quit his hedge fund day job, moved to California, and now he and his nonprofit have 6,000 videos online that have been viewed over 468 million times (Khan Academy, 2014). Each of the videos is free to anyone with an Internet connection. The topics lean more heavily toward math and science, but other areas are growing as well.

But then what? Teachers have to think about how material can be taught using a problem set or interactive assignment in the classroom. You also have to remember that as with any homework, simply assigning it will not be enough. Will the students actually watch the video, and how will you ensure they do? After you learn how to create your own video, this chapter will give you suggestions to tackle this issue.

One other issue to be cognizant of is to know which of your students can watch the video at home. Any student with a smartphone or an Internet connection can view the video. However, for the few students who don't have access to the Internet in their homes, you might want to provide a list of local libraries or see if the student can come to your classroom to view the lecture during lunch or after school before the lesson is applied in class.

If the goal is to have students learn at a pace that is reasonably best for them, flipping gives teachers much more latitude than they have ever had. Consider when students miss a week of school because of an illness or they change schools in the middle of the academic year. Typically they start wherever the teacher is and, at some point, make up the work. But this makes as much sense as starting a novel in the middle and going back later to read the first few chapters. If all of your lectures are available as videos, then the recorded lessons can become the anchor to a self-paced classroom. The video then becomes the anchor to your learning module, followed by a hands-on lesson. Some students will be able to work more quickly, while others, who need remediation, can receive additional help from the teacher in class. This model allows for one-on-one learning time between the teacher and the student. No longer do you have to wait for a scheduled review period: You can now have students progressing at various paces simultaneously in one classroom. What is even more important is that flipping allows you to throw out standardized pacing, where all students have to be working in lockstep format. Now you can create learning modules and let students work at their own pace. For example, a student could choose to work ahead and finish a course early. Likewise struggling students have the chance to work more carefully to fully learn the class concepts. That being said, flipping a classroom is not an excuse for a lazy student not to do work in a timely fashion.

> If all of your lectures are available as videos, then the recorded lessons can become the anchor to a self-paced classroom.

To summarize, the benefits of flipping can include, but aren't limited to

- a video that summarizes and connects the main points about what needs to be taught,
- a hands-on classroom activity where the teacher can move around the room helping anyone who needs help, and
- individualized lesson plans so that those who want to move more quickly through various lessons can do just that.

WHAT TO FLIP

To say you should take your current PowerPoints and break them down into segments of video for your students would be to miss the point. You might want to think first of what is going to be done in class and then make a flipped video of the background needed to prepare for that work. If, for example, you were looking at William Golding's *Lord of the Flies*, you might want to give students an exercise looking at the main points that Golding was trying to make and his view of our society. These would be tough questions that students might need assistance in understanding. A flipped video on Golding's life and how he was led to his beliefs and the subsequent writing of his book would be a good topic for your video. This video could even include the short clip found online of Golding discussing his own thoughts.

Once you have your lesson and the video idea ready, you will have to line up what you need for the flipped overview. I usually include a few Presentation slides, since written words often help student comprehension. I also have additional tabs set up on my browser. Perhaps a very short clip from the *Lord of the Flies* movie might enhance your presentation as would a picture of Golding. Once these assets are set up, it will be easy to move through the parts of the video, remembering that it is okay to have bloopers as students seem to like it when their teachers appear more human in a video. Adding in personal touches also makes the videos more interesting for your students. My own children have all had cameos in my instructional videos as have the family pets!

Lastly, it is important to note that it is okay to use videos from other educators as long as they fit your needs. Use your Twitter/Google+/ Google search engines to look for flipped videos on your topic. Ask your Twitter followers for recommendations, or send a message to someone with a large Twitter following to see if they can help point you in the right direction. There is a growing library of short videos on the Internet that you can add to your digital library by bookmarking them for later use.

MAKING YOUR OWN SCREENCAST

To make a flipped video, the best software to use is from the website screencast-o-matic.com. As with everything in this book, it is free and easily accessed on the Internet. While you can set up your own account, you do not need do so. Making a screencast means that everything on the screen including your voice will be captured on the video. Here are the steps to follow.

- Screencast-O-Matic videos are saved on YouTube, so before you begin to make a video, log onto YouTube. If you have never used YouTube, you will be asked a few simple questions and will then be set to start your video.
- Set up your browser tabs for your lecture.
- When you are ready to record, go to screencast-o-matic.com.
- Tap the "Record" button on lower left side of the page. You will be asked if you want to download the java script (which is code to

make a program run). Say "yes," as it is safe for your laptop. You may be prompted several times, but each time say "yes."

- Then a window will pop up, and you will tap the "Run" button to run the java script.
- A dotted line rectangle will then appear. You will be able to put your cursor at one of the edges on the white box, and an arrow that you can drag in or out will appear. Make the dotted-line box large enough to include the web pages you will be using. Make sure to leave about an inch at the bottom of your screen so you can hit the record and stop buttons. In addition to web pages, your screencast video can include Google Drive Presentations.

- The next decision you will have to make is whether or not to include your image in the screencast. If you do want to include video of yourself, you need to click the arrow in the lower left side of the screen and make sure the "FaceTime Camera" is on.
- Drag your own image to the corner of your screen so it is out of the way, knowing that you can adjust it when the screencast is done.
- When you are ready to begin, click on the red circle on the lower left side of your screen, and you will be given a 3, 2, 1 count to start recording. At any time you can stop and restart. For your first attempt, record for a few seconds, stop, and hit the play button to see if the volume is okay. Then push "restart" and start the process again. Keep the entire screencast video to ten minutes or less, and remember to speak slowly as your students will be taking notes.

- If you want to stop so that you can go from one online resource to another, hit the pause button on the lower left side.
- Once you are finished with the entire video, click "done" and then "publish to YouTube." Be sure to give it a descriptive name so it is easy for others to find, and then hit the upload button. It is often best to name the video for the module you are covering in class, as in "Comparative and Absolute Advantage."
- The video will then do something called encoding (which means it is being digitized) and then will be uploaded to YouTube. The entire process will take about as long to complete as the video is long (i.e., approximately ten minutes).
- If you want more help, watch the tutorial on the Screencast-O-Matic site.
- Once your video has been fully uploaded to YouTube, you will be given a link to it, which you can put into your class platform such as Blackboard, Edmodo, or Google Sites (more on these in Chapter 6).

CREATING A YOUTUBE PLAYLIST

You will want to organize your YouTube account so that your students (or PLC members) can easily access your videos. To do this, take the following steps.

- Log onto your Google account and go to the YouTube icon/site.
- Click on My Channel from the left side menu.
- Click on Video Manager.
- Click on Playlist. If you do not have one, go to the right side of the page and click on the "+" beside "New playlist."
- Then fill in your new playlist title and click "Create playlist."
- Once you have created a playlist, then you "Add video by URL," which means you simply have to paste the hyperlink into the space. Then make sure you press "Done" on the upper right side. You can add your own URLs here or anyone else's that you find in YouTube. If you want to see any example of a playlist, type in "Ken Halla" in YouTube and you will find mine.
- You will then have one URL for the entire collection, which you can share with your students or PLC.
- If you want to use videos from other people, copy the URL, go to the edit button, and add it on the list just as you would your own.
- If you want to change the order of your list, put your cursor beside the number of each video, and a "+" sign will appear. Then just drag each video up or down.

Visit http://bit.ly/digitalclassroomteacherguide to access live links.

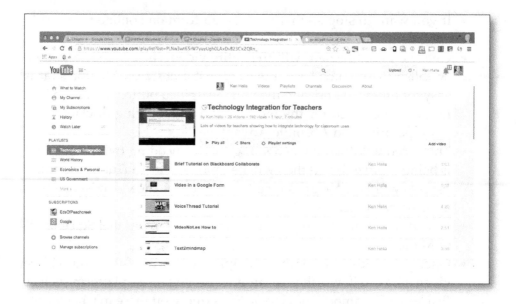

Another way to "give" your students the list of videos is to simply create a Google Drive document with each of the links on it. This could be tailored for each unit or each class. Even better, you could then insert a link into the class platform. The advantage of linking the videos this way is that the teacher can edit the video list on the Google Drive document without having to go into the class platform.

LEARNING FROM A FLIPPED VIDEO LECTURE

How do you get your students to watch the videos? You may have a few who won't, but unfortunately that is true of most assignments. By looking at the number of views underneath the video you will get a rough idea how many students are actually watching the videos. Here are some ideas for how to motivate students to watch the videos.

- Create a Google Drive Form, and require students to post questions about the topic. You will be amazed how this gives voice to so many students who are usually reticent in class. The day after the video is assigned, begin class by sharing students' questions. You will notice students' confidence growing as they see their classmates nodding in approval to their questions. I find that it is a safe forum for student participation since the questions are submitted anonymously, allowing students to be completely honest.
- Give students a short quiz the day following the video assignment. Allow students to use their notes on the assessment. The assessment

could be a simple five-question quiz covering the main points, questions from a released state exam, or questions from an old Advanced Placement exam. Allowing students to use their notes will motivate them either to take good notes or at least to watch the video closely.

- Place the video in a Google Drive form (instructions are below), and ask questions below the video as you would in any survey.

Video Not.es

Note taking will be more effective if you encourage students to take notes digitally. Students can store the notes in their Google Drive folders and use them later as study guides. Teach students to split their computer screen to show the video and their notes at the same time. Alternatively, they can toggle back and forth from the video tab to the Google Drive tab. The newest app students can use is VideoNot.es. Videonot.es allows you to see a YouTube video on the left side of your screen and to write on a document on the right side.

- To access VideoNot.es, students need to go into Google Drive and to the "New" icon in the upper left.
- Then go to "connect more apps." Search for VideoNot.es. Once you tap on it, it will ask if you agree to share your login information with Google Drive. Say yes!
- Once you are in VideoNot.es, your screen will be split.
- Have your students paste in the URL of your video from YouTube.

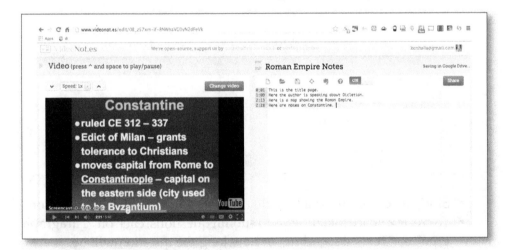

- Put the title where it says "Here is your title."
- Below the title students can take notes as the video plays. The cool thing is that when students go back to the highlighted time stamp beside the note (see image above), the program will rewind the video back to the point where that note was taken.

Visit http://bit.ly/digitalclassroomteacherguide to access live links.

- To see their Videonot.es in Google Drive, students should go to the "Recent" tab on the lower left side. Then the student can right click on the name of the item and go to "Move" and put it in the appropriate folder.
- One negative is that the notes cannot be organized in Cornell fashion. If you would prefer that students take Cornell-style notes, have them copy and paste their notes into a Google Drive document.

Student Questions

- To get students to submit questions anonymously about the contents of your flipped video, set up a Google Forms questionnaire.
- Go to your Google Drive page and hit "New" > "More > "Forms." You will then be prompted to title your form. You will be offered a variety of backgrounds. After you have made your selection, your screen will look like the image below. The title will be the name of your flipped video.
- Go to "Insert" and "video" and type in the name of your video. If you do not know the name, you can tap on the left where it says "URL" and use the YouTube search bar to find your video.

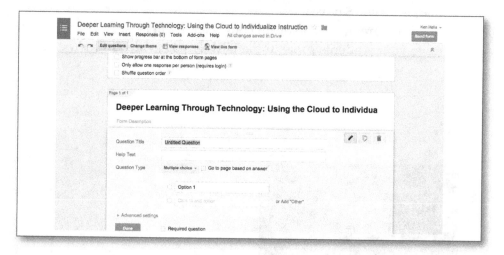

- Students do not need a Google Drive account to submit a question.
- To create a space for students to submit questions, click on "Paragraph type" or "Text" depending on how long the question will be.
- Since not every student will have a question, you do not need to make it a "required question."
- Alternatively you could give each student several fill-in-the-blank or multiple-choice questions, and require them to respond to see if the students actually watched the video.

- After each question is created, hit the "Done" button.
- To add more questions, hit the "Add item" drop down.
- When you are done, hit "View live form" at the top of the page. On the live form, you will be given a URL, which you can give to your students so that they can complete the assignment.

In a typical class of thirty, you will get between thirteen and fifteen questions that will generate a useful class discussion the next day. To start the discussion,

- go to the top of the Google form where you created the questions and click on the "View responses" tab;
- click on the "A" in the column marked "A" so that the entire column is highlighted, right click and hit the "Hide column" tab for the time stamp; and
- project your computer screen onto the board or wall of your classroom.

THE FLIPPED CLASSROOM

What comes next should be every student's dream come true. When I was in school, I was pretty good at listening to my math teachers explain how to do math problems. I was usually able to complete the first few problems of the homework assignment in class. However, when I got home and tried to complete the rest of the problem set, I ran into difficulties since the back of the math textbook included answers to only the even questions. It seemed like I could never figure out the odd ones on my own. In contrast, in a flipped class, students spend class time working on hands-on projects such as problem sets, interactive lessons, challenging group projects, or other hands-on assignments that often require

Visit http://bit.ly/digitalclassroomteacherguide to access live links.

some intermittent help from the teacher. For students who need more clarification after viewing the video lecture, flipped class time allows teachers to offer help on an individual basis. Teachers might even have the time to work with students who are falling behind. Outside of school, students are already learning using this model when they are working on mastering a computer game or on how to use their cell phones. They learn by trial and error and then, when needed, consult with their friends. Take advantage of the class time opportunities to push your students to higher levels of thinking (think Bloom's taxonomy). In Chapter 5 we will learn how to create assignments for students in the classroom. Interactive assignments can be adapted for different learning abilities and different learning styles. They are the type of assignment you might want to match with a flipped video.

> In a flipped class, students spend class time working on hands-on projects such as problem sets, interactive lessons, challenging group projects, or other hands-on assignments that often require some intermittent help from the teacher.

The more advanced and more motivated students will have class time to get ahead if given the option. They might choose to finish the course a month or two ahead of schedule. Or they might enjoy the opportunity of tutoring their more challenged peers. Peer-to-peer tutoring accomplishes at least two goals. First, it reinforces the learning of the advanced student and, second, it provides teachers with an in-class assistant (or two) to better reach all of the students in the classroom. Finally teachers can still use their traditional groups with different levels and types of learners in each group. As with the more capable learner above, this will create groups where the students' individual strengths can help one another and move everyone forward together.

As you are adjusting to this new teaching style, remember that your students are also adjusting and will not adapt overnight. Given that the teacher is allowing Internet devices or even just space to work on one's own, the educator is going to have to move around the classroom a great deal to ensure on-task behavior. No more will there be a front of the room, but rather just a location where the teacher happens to be working. The teacher will also have to learn which students are the most effective at completing their tasks and who has to be prodded more often. This means grouping students who can help one another. To be effective, teachers need to completely rethink all of their lessons to make sure that they are using the strengths of the students and guiding the students to learn better and retain the material longer.

FLIPPED CLASS RESOURCES

The flipped classroom idea has been growing very quickly in the United States. It works for elementary school students as well as for medical school students. A proliferation of resources have become available to teachers.

Flipped Video Collections

- For math teachers, the largest sites are <u>Khan Academy</u> and <u>Mathispower4u</u>.
- For the humanities, go to <u>Knowmia</u>, which has more than 13,000 videos.
- <u>Teacher Tube</u> is a well-established site that started in 2007 and now has more than 400,000 videos.
- <u>PBS Teachers' page</u>, <u>National Geographic</u>, and <u>Smithsonian</u> are also great resources.
- For each of these sites, you can follow the Twitter and Google+ tags. Following the tags to your favorite sites will lead you to many other wonderful resources. It's also a good idea to bookmark the sites where you would want to return.

PLCs for Flippers

Flipping a classroom will open your world to a whole new series of videos, hashtags, and Google searches. For example, if you type "#flipclass" into Google+ you will be connected instantly with hundreds of other educators exploring and trying out flipping in their classes.

- If you prefer Twitter, you can also go to "#flipclass" every Monday evening from 8:00 to 9:00 p.m. EST to take part in a discussion on teaching a flipped class.
- Some of the most well known and prolific flipped educators who share are included in the list below along with their Twitter handles.
  - Jon Bergmann, Science @jonbergmann
  - Aaron Sams, Science @chemicalsams
  - Brian Bennett, Science @bennettscience
  - Phil McIntosh, Math @mistermcintosh
  - April Gudenrath, English @agudteach
  - Ramsey Musallam, Science @ramusallam
  - Jason Kern, Civics @jasonmkern
  - David Fouch, Social Studies @davidfouch

    o Ken Halla, Social Studies @kenhalla
    o Karl Lindgren-Streicher, History @LS_Karl
    o Tara Becker-Utess, Government @t_becker10
    o Stacey Roshan, Math @buddyxo
    o Steve Kelly, Math @bigkxcountry
    o Dan Muscarella, Math @danmuscarella
    o Kristin Daniels, Technology @kadaniels
    o Lindsay Cole, Biology @lindsaybcole
    o Cheryl Morris, English @guster4lovers
    o Andrew Thomasson, English @thomasson_engl

Source: Spencer, 2013.

- There are also many web pages you can use, starting with Flipped-Learning.com.
- Even more popular, at 10,000 members strong in 2013, is the Flipped Learning Network (flippedlearning.org). The network has lists of different groups you can join, covering all levels of instruction as well as content. It also has forums where you can ask other educators for help and videos. It is an essential site if you are going to join the flipped world.
- Another great resource is the Flipped Learning Journal (flipped learningjournal.org), which has aggregated a number of teachers around the country who collaborate on flipped projects. You will also find an incredible number of e-mails, Twitter links, and videos from educators around the country at that site.

Who knows where the flipping will go? In addition to its free videos, the Khan Academy started an initiative in early 2013 in Idaho with 10,000 students in 47 schools. After giving teachers a two-day, in-service training, the educators quickly noticed how students who were weak in a subject were watching videos multiple times and others who learned more quickly were moving ahead at a faster rate ("Khan Academy Founder Heralds Nation's First Statewide Pilot in Idaho," 2013). The Khan Academy is now using algorithms for its partner schools to see how to best implement its videos in the classroom. This means that the more people the nonprofit follows, the more information will be collected and the better the service can become. The Khan program gives students problem sets and assesses whether students have mastered a topic; if not, it suggests new videos to watch. It even gives hints to students who do not get a problem correct. Since teachers have access to all the students' work done for the partner Khan Academy schools, they can see if several students are having trouble on the same concept and, if necessary, bring them together for a minitutorial. Thus it completely individualizes the material so the teacher can move around and work as a facilitator and motivator.

To see the links in this chapter, use your smartphone and the QR box below. Alternatively, you can go to http://bit.ly/digitalclassroomteacherguide, if you prefer to use your laptop.

CLASSROOM EXAMPLES

There is no shortage of ways you can utilize the flipped model. While the most common option might be moving some of the instruction outside the classroom (to the home, library, etc.), there are also ways to utilize the model in class. Consider my ESOL students, many of whom do not have Internet in their homes. To help them, I bought ten cheap headphones for those who did not have their own earbuds and started flipping within the class. Since that meant that the students were not getting through our material adequately, some of them started visiting my class at lunchtime once a week, bringing their lunches with them and eating while they watched the videos.

Because of the language barrier, many of my ESOL students often had to watch the videos over and over until they could answer questions based on the content. Having flipped videos allowed my students not only to watch the lecture multiple times but also to avoid, what for them would be, asking embarrassing questions.

Another reason for using the flipped model is not to lose instruction time on snow days. I tell my students that snow day means "at home work day." When we get the word that school is canceled, I send them a Remind text with a shortened link (addressed in Chapter 7) to the flipped video and assignment written on a Google Drive document. I also set up a folder in Google Drive that contains the work assignment and make the folder available to my students. Students without Internet access at home have the opportunity of catching up over the next several class periods, but most students without Internet at home have access to at least one smartphone in their house and can therefore watch a flipped video or visit a website.

You can also have the students become the teachers and make their own flipped videos. If the idea of a flipped video is to focus on the most important part of a topic of study, then why not make your students do the same thing? My world history students have used free online resources to make video interviews of immigrant members of their families. Each student then writes an essay and creates a video diary detailing their family member's story, as well showing the connection from the family member to what we have been learning in class.

(Continued)

(Continued)

The result is always a great product, which I can usually use as a teaching tool for other students as a means of introducing eras we cover in class. The students' videos help explain to other students why learning world history can be so important and pertinent to their own personal lives and family histories.

It helps to think beyond your content, which for me is social studies. However, one of my most successful flipped videos is one I made on how to write an essay. It seems odd to me that explaining it in class would not be as effective, but there was a notable improvement in students' writing after they watched the video. Creating the video offered me a forum to show a well-written thesis, topic sentences, use of facts, and other important elements of an essay. Students were able to stop the video to read and contemplate on these elements in a way that was much more effective than my delivering a lecture to everyone at once. The first time I used the essay video, my class of thirty viewed it 150 times, telling me they needed multiple views to make sure they had fully grasped all of the elements covered.

One final note is that I suggest you find a partner to work with who will offer you honest feedback on your videos and helpful suggestions on how to improve your class assignments. In return, you could offer the same feedback to your partner.

EDUCATOR CHALLENGES

Monday Morning Challenge: Create a five- to ten-minute video lesson using Screencast-O-Matic. Be simple in your first attempt and just use Presentation slides. Once you have done this, create a YouTube playlist and make this video the first one on your list.

Tuesday Morning Challenge: Once your video is done, share it with your PLC and ask for feedback on what method you might use to follow the video: student questions, class discussion, background for a reading, and so on. It would be even better if one of your PLC members would agree to flip with you so that you two can give each other daily support.

Wednesday Morning Challenge: Create a second video using items other than Presentation slides. In addition to a few slides that include keywords, add images or video clips.

Thursday Morning Challenge: Find one or two collections of flipped videos that you might use in your classroom. Assign one of the videos to your students, following up with an assignment of your own creation.

Friday Morning Challenge: Use Twitter to share your new flipped videos with your followers. If you use the word "flip" or "flipped classroom" in your Tweet, you will notice other flippers on the middle left of your page under the tag "Who to Follow."

Twitter Hashtag Challenge: Share the sites for videos you have discovered by tweeting about them on #individualizelearning. Share the flipped videos you have developed. You might want to include a second hashtag (#algegra, #ushistory, #langarts) so people in your content area will be more likely to find your Tweet.

5

Interactive Assignments

- Learn how to create interactive assignments, applying Bloom's taxonomy
- Find resources for creating interactives
- Learn how to create rubrics for assessing interactives

This chapter is meant to be a guide of suggestions and thoughts about how you can use what you have learned in this book to tailor your classroom to meet the individual learning needs of your students. As with any of the suggestions in this book, start with one class or content area and expand to more as you become increasingly comfortable with the new teaching techniques.

CREATING INTERACTIVE ASSIGNMENTS

Interactive Learning and Its Benefits Defined

This book is designed so that each chapter builds on previous ones. You have learned how to build a virtual professional learning community, how to use Google Drive, how to utilize online resources, and then how to make flipped videos. This chapter will focus on the classroom portion of a flipped class, which involves interactive learning as opposed to passive learning when students listen while the teacher talks.

> The goal is to help move a student along the path toward deeper learning.

So what is an "interactive"? My definition is that it is any lesson where students receive continuous feedback from the teacher and/or other students in the classroom. As students work on the more difficult parts of a lesson, they can seek out peer and teacher assistance. Thus there is interaction with both other people as well as the content. Know, though, that feedback is not the same as giving out answers. The goal is to help move a student along the path toward deeper learning. This may involve reteaching, leading by questioning, or checking for understanding. It often involves some level of higher-thinking skills. So for example, an interactive could be a math problem set, an art project, writing an essay, or completing a group project such as a science experiment. Students who are working on these types of assignments benefit from having access to a teacher so that they can ask both simple and more complex questions. The key is that the teacher is interacting with the students and providing feedback right away, rather than a student's going home and becoming frustrated by being unable to complete an assignment without assistance.

Technology can be a useful tool for creating interactive assignments. Think about essay writing as an example. A teacher can give feedback right away by walking around the room from student to student or by using Google Drive documents to give feedback on student essays. For example, if the immediate goal is to write a thesis, then the teacher can make comments in students' Google Drive documents in real time while sitting at a desk in the classroom. This is actually quicker than walking around the classroom. Comments and edits made to Google Drive documents appear immediately, so students don't need to wait for feedback. This means you can quickly grade student work in class, insert comments when necessary, and even call students over when a student problem is best handled by a face-to-face conversation. Students who have worked ahead at their own pace can be available to help their peers.

As has been stated many times before, not all students learn the same way. One way to provide differentiation for students at different levels might be to ask your English Speakers of Other Language (ESOL) students to look up definitions for words that might seem basic to native speakers. As another example, not all students need to remain limited to the five-paragraph essay. If some students have mastered essay writing early in the year, challenge them to advance by requiring them to include more in-depth essays. The types of interactive assignments you assign after a flipped video are limitless. It should be noted that interactive work often involves higher-level thinking skills, and hence some students might need help (from teacher or peers) with the more difficult work.

Student Reading Levels

Your students will be reading a wide variety of material from textbooks to newspapers, websites, and so forth. To assume they can all read and comprehend at the same level would be a mistake. In the beginning of the year or semester, it would be a good idea to ascertain their reading levels by administering some sort of reading assessment. The reading assessment should be revised and readministered midway through the year to gauge the improvement students have made. ESOL students, for example, are most likely to miss questions on standardized tests not because they do not know the subject material but rather because they do not know the English vernacular used in the questions. To understand the reading levels of your students, you can use a number of free online assessments. One of these is Mind Sprinting. This test is fairly quick, free, and can be done in an hour. It will give you an approximate reading ability for each of your students at the beginning of the year. There are other tests available online, which you can find by doing a search for "free reading test."

Textbook Reading Levels

Now that you have a sense of your students' reading levels, you need to assess the lexile complexity of the class textbook and other class reading assignments. If your textbook or other reading assignments are in digital format, there are multiple ways you can find out the reading level (or lexile complexity). Lexile complexity is measured by various instruments. Some of these include Flesch-Kincaid, Gunning Fog Index, SMOG Index, Fry Readability Formula, and Coleman-Liau indices.

- The Readability Test Tool and the Juicy Test allow the user to input a URL and get an immediate level.
- But the definitive test is probably the one from R. M. Felder of NC State. When you run the test, it will tell you both the reading level of the text as well as the most appropriate age for the students who are to read it.
- Many textbooks' older versions can be found online, or at the very least you can try to go to Google Books or Amazon (since most textbooks have an e-copy of the first chapter online) and find a digital snippet that will help you assess the reading level.
- Another alternative is simply to Google something like "Flesch-Kincaid + textbook title." This should give you a score to let you know if the lexile complexity matches the reading level of most of your students. If necessary, type a few paragraphs of the reading

material into an online Flesch-Kincaid site to see what level of lexile complexity the instrument assigns to the text.

Learning Styles

In addition to displaying a span of reading levels, your students will also display an array of learning styles. One way to look at learning styles is through the Felder-Silverman model that breaks learning into five types: "auditory, abstract (intuitive), deductive, passive, and sequential" (Felder & Silverman, 1988, p. 680). The original 1988 Felder-Silverman paper that espoused the breakdown is one of the most cited models among academics, getting about 100,000 hits a year online (<u>Felder & Silverman, 1988</u>). Felder's <u>web page</u> has a plethora of articles you can read if you want to explore this topic in more depth. You can find the link on this book's list of links or by going to a search engine and typing in "Richard Felder Resources in Science and Engineering Education." For a good overview, check out the 1988 paper, where Richard Felder and Linda Silverman detail not only learning styles but also corresponding teaching methodologies that one might use in the classroom for each style. Felder and Silverman look at several "modes of learning," all of which advocate using student interactives rather than passive lecture to nurture intellectual development. The authors conclude that

- students prefer to receive information through "sights, sounds, insights, and hunches" as well as through "pictures, diagrams, graphs, demonstrations, words, and sounds" (Felder & Silverman, 1988, p. 675);
- students process information best through reflective activities or learning by doing; and
- students master understanding best through a step-by-step process or in a take-one-step-back-and-look-at-the-big-picture methodology.

Once you have assessed your students' reading levels, you can choose the corresponding teaching strategies that will best accommodate their learning. Felder and Silverman identify three learning modalities: visual, auditory, and kinesthetic. Essentially they argue that people best suited for auditory learning lose information when it is presented in only a visual format. In other words, auditory learners need to hear instructions or content information. Likewise, visual learners need to see pictures, diagrams, flow charts, and so on, to better learn and retain information. Given this information, think about how you can improve your presentations in class. Do you simply present slides that contain a lot of words, or do you also include pictures and other visuals to highlight the information? What about audio files or video? You might use the 10–2 model for auditory learners, for example, so they can process their learning by listening. This is where the learner listens to a flipped video, for example, for ten minutes and then discusses the material. The student could work with the teacher or another student who is moving at the same speed and repeat the most important information, summarizing what has been said and how the information is connected to previously learned material (Fredericks, 2013). The key here is that you do not need to use the 10–2 method for every student. If you are using interactives, the students who do not need the 10–2 method can continue learning or use a different methodology.

Felder and Silverman (1988) argue that the kinesthetic learner needs to learn through active participation. Think about how well you have learned the content that you teach—this is largely due to the fact that you spent time devising lesson plans, finding supplementary documents, discussing the material with others—in short, learning kinesthetically. Keeping that in mind when you plan activities for your students, make sure you incorporate lessons that involve learning by doing.

> Felder and Silverman (1988) argue that the kinesthetic learner needs to learn through active participation.

None of us falls totally into one category or another. All learners will benefit if learning material is presented in a variety of formats rather than primarily in one.

Bloom's Taxonomy

Adapting your teaching to the individual needs of your students involves much more than simply listening to a child's preferences and adopting a lesson plan to please the student. Your more successful students are likely to be the ones who prefer the lecture and regurgitation methods of teaching. These are the students who have thrived in traditional methods of schooling. When asked, they will not want to change what works well for them. However, it may be that these students are not as successful at retaining information over long periods of time, or it may be that they can increase retention by being exposed to various teaching styles. Additionally, different approaches to learning will likely help students succeed when they are faced with more open-ended exercises where they are given some academic freedom that challenges their independent thinking.

One of the hardest things to do as a teacher in the Internet age is to let go of the teaching methods that helped you as a student. Most teachers were good students and still enjoy learning—hence their career path. The longest-serving teachers tend to be the ones who are continually learning new content and rethinking their teaching strategies.

To help us consider different techniques we can use in the classroom, let us look at Bloom's taxonomy, which postulates that students must learn some basic knowledge. Then they have to be able to apply it in different ways, moving up an increasingly more thoughtful ladder of learning. Bloom's taxonomy was first proposed in 1956 and, more recently, was updated in 2000.

1956	2000	Simple Definition from the Bloom Wheel
Knowledge	Remember	This is simple memorizing—think definitions.
Comprehension	Understand	This would involve asking students questions to see if they learned basic concepts.
Application	Apply	Creating a demonstration, sculpture, illustration, presentation, interview, performance, etc.
Analysis	Analyze	Looking at documents, videos, books, Venn diagram, etc., and summarizing or coming up with main points.
Evaluation	Evaluate	Making a judgment based on something learned—set up a debate, blog, mind maps, etc.
Synthesis	Create	This happens when the student creates something entirely new from the learning such as a hypothesis, scientific experiment, a video, a journal entry from a different perspective, etc.

Google "Bloom's Digital Taxonomy Wheel and Knowledge Dimension" (see below) to find an even better representation of the depth of learning than the one shown above. This is the type of depth of learning that you should be exposing your students to each day. The website is an amazing online resource that shows you several strategies you can use in the classroom. When you click on a section, several methodologies will briefly appear in the chart (Edutechology, 2013). It will be a stupendous resource for you in your classroom and should definitely be added to your online bookmarks so you can refer to the site time and time again.

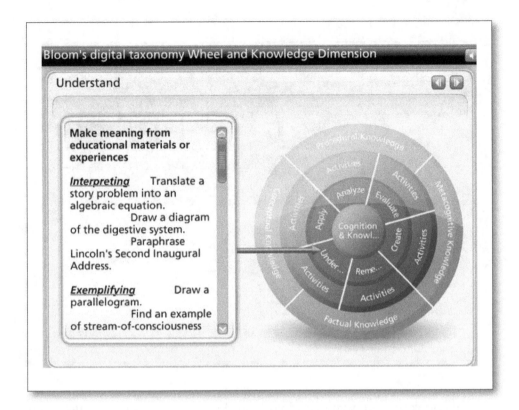

RESOURCES FOR CREATING INTERACTIVE ASSIGNMENTS

Fakebook, Faketweet, Faketext

One way to apply the upper levels of Bloom's is to consider using FakeTweet, FakeText, and Fakebook, which were put together by British teacher Russel Tarr (@russeltarr). They are a good alternative to assignments involving Twitter, Facebook, and real texting. Fakebook looks exactly like Facebook (and FakeTweet like Twitter, etc.) and will therefore be enticing to your students because of its familiarity. Asking students to summarize the learning material into short Fakebook posts or even shorter FakeTweet comments will require them to identify the essential elements of the content and, therefore, will necessitate synthesis.

You might ask your students to carry on a fictional conversation between authors on Fakebook discussing two novels you have read in class. Likewise, you could ask students to show you what a conversation between various scientists might look like.

Visit http://bit.ly/digitalclassroomteacherguide to access live links.

Fakebook will allow you and your students to create unique URLs and profiles without having to surrender any personal information.

- When you go the Fakebook page, there is a translucent overlay that shows you where items you are going to add should go. From there it is almost self-explanatory.
- To create a profile page on Fakebook, enter the name of the person where it says "Click here to enter name." The site will ask for a photo of the person. You can either upload a class photo, a student's self-portrait, or any other image of the student's choosing.
- You can then enter a post ("Add post," which is right below the image of your person) or a series of them. There is even a comment tab below each post. Likewise you can add famous historical figures and tag them as your Fakebook friends on the left side of the page. After entering in each of the names, their images will appear.
- Once the student has entered in all of the relevant information, go to the top right side and click "Save."
- The site will then ask for a code, which I tell my students to enter as their last name or the name of their school.
- The site will give the student a unique URL. You might suggest that the student put both the link and their password on a Google Drive document so it is not forgotten.

- Finally, you will notice there is a Fakebook how-to video in the middle of the screen on the website, in case you need more help.

As with the other applications and tools in this book, going to YouTube to search for a tutorial is an easy way to learn more if you need more help.

Free Textbook Resources Online

Online textbook materials are a great resource when you are creating interactive assignments for students. Most major textbook companies often offer review material online for their textbooks. Google the name of your textbook, adding "+ ancillaries" to the search. You may not find ancillaries for the current version of your textbook, but the learning materials will be a good start to providing online resources to your students. For example, you could include links to the online resources when you create student assignments. Often the ancillaries include useful summaries of the material you are studying. This means that you might have the students look at a map or a math problem tutorial from the ancillary. This could be built into your interactive assignment. Assuming you are using Google Drive documents, you could easily link the assignment to the ancillary. You might also find formative assessment quizzes, which students can take over and over until they master a subject. In your continued efforts to encourage your students to be self-paced, offer extra review materials to help those who aren't performing well on formative assessments.

Hippocampus

Another good resource is <u>Hippocampus</u>, which has e-textbooks for most standard high school classes at both the standard and AP levels including biology, chemistry, physics, earth science, economics, history, psychology, English, and religion. Their textbooks include video breakdowns of the subjects, are very professionally made, and, as with everything in this book, the site is free.

In some places, like chemistry, Hippocampus has been married to the Khan Academy so that you can look for your subject's accepted content and find a video to go with each topic. Likewise, in physics you also find an outline of the course with lectures, but there will also be "Physics in the Real World" videos, so your students can see real-life applications. So Hippocampus could be used either in a flipped classroom or as a way to tutor students who want more review.

Visit http://bit.ly/digitalclassroomteacherguide to access live links.

Wikipedia

Although some teachers discourage the use of Wikipedia in academic set-tings, one 2010 study queried 2,500 college students and found that almost every student started his or her research with Wikipedia. Wikipedia receives nineteen billion page views a month, making it the number-five hit website on the Internet (Grathwohl, 2011). Several studies have agreed that Wikipedia is very accurate including a well-known *Nature* magazine article in 2005 that found Wikipedia comparable in accuracy to *Encyclopedia Britannica* (Wolchover, 2011). What tends to scare educators regarding its accuracy is the fact that articles can be changed by anyone. On the other hand, there are 80,000 volunteers updating the site to make sure the infor-mation is correct ("Why Does Wikipedia Work?" 2014).

The more you explore Wikipedia, the more you will find it to be a use-ful addition to your classroom resources. You could use portions of a Wikipedia entry (include the link) to supplement your students' textbook so as to add more depth and nuance to a given topic. As you move from section to section in a Wikipedia entry, you will notice that the URL changes slightly. If you want your students to look only at a particular section, be sure to get the link for the exact location of that section. You can easily find the links by looking at the "Contents" right under the introductory summary. Click on one of the sections and you will see a new URL in your browser. For an example of an interactive assignment involving links to these sources, please see the end of this chapter under "Classroom Examples."

Interactive assignments are meant to be updated on a regular basis. No longer should you be tied to a static textbook, but rather the textbook should be only one of many resources you use—some of which might be a link to part of a Wikipedia article, a video from Hippocampus, a link to a section in an online textbook ancillary, an interview with an expert in a field, or any number of other resources. For example, recently I came across a short video comparing Schoolhouse Rock's "I'm Just a Bill on Capitol Hill" (Frishberg, 1975) to a smartly made video by the online news source Vox showing the way a bill really becomes a law (Posner, 2014). After watching the video, I went on Google Drive, found my interactive assignment on the topic, added in the "How a Bill Really Becomes Law: What Schoolhouse Rock Missed," as well as several questions on the new video, and in minutes, I had updated my assignment. In addition, I did not have to log into the school learning platform (something you will learn about in Chapter 6), delete the old assignment, and upload the new one because the platform contained the link to my online Google Drive assign-ment. Once I had updated my Google Drive document, the platform led students to the updated assignment. Even better, I was able to make the update months before my students were to work on the lesson.

Create Your Own eBooks!

If your students have Apple devices, consider creating your own ebook with iBook Author. Just as I have outlined above, iBook allows you to create and constantly update your own "home grown" textbooks. This will allow you to tailor your own book to your specific needs. Think of it as a yearlong PLC challenge! Even better, have your students create books for themselves. This might sound a bit far-fetched, but if you want to see if students, working cooperatively, have learned a topic, creating a book might be a wonderful and engaging assessment of their learned knowledge. It would also allow for multiple modalities to be used to meet the learning needs of all readers. It could also be improved by students in subsequent years.

The iBook app comes complete with easy-to-build, premade templates. The app allows users to upload images, video, and text. Google "Apple iBook" to find a site explaining how to create your own book. The books are so easy to create that most elementary students can do it. On the Bloom's taxonomy chart, students' application of knowledge to create their own ebooks using multimedia sources would rank at the highest level. The only downside of iBook Author is that your students have to have an Apple device to create it.

RUBRICS

If you are going to use thoughtful, interactive assignments, you will need to develop rubrics to grade them. To ensure that the assessment process is transparent to your students from the get-go, they should be handed the rubric at the same time the assignment is given out. It is always helpful to go over the rubric with your students before they begin the assignment. The rubric should be the guide for students as they go about completing an assignment. As with any interactive, showing an example of a completed assignment is also helpful to serve as a model for students.

> It is always helpful to go over the rubric with your students before they begin the assignment.

You will be able to find many rubrics posted on the Internet. As with earlier learning in this book, if you need help, just go to Google and search for something like "art poster rubric" and see what comes up. You will find not only rubrics in your search results but also assignments that fit that description.

A good tool for creating rubrics is the site <u>Rubistar</u>. You do not need to join Rubistar to use it. Go to the "Create a rubric" tab in the upper right hand corner to get started. Rubistar allows you to create your own rubrics simply by answering its questions. It also has rubric makers for every content area in education, so it is a place you may return to time and time again. Rubistar asks you to select a category and then asks you a series of questions using drop-down menus. When you have finished, you will have created a rubric that you can use for your students.

One last point to consider with using rubrics, like many other types of assignments, is how you define mastery. I often have my students share their assignments with me as they are progressing so they can receive feedback as they work on their projects. If you are operating in a self-paced environment, you can also have students make changes once the entire assignment is complete. If the goal is to learn, requiring that the students make suggested improvements is far more productive than accepting the submission of incomplete or inferior work.

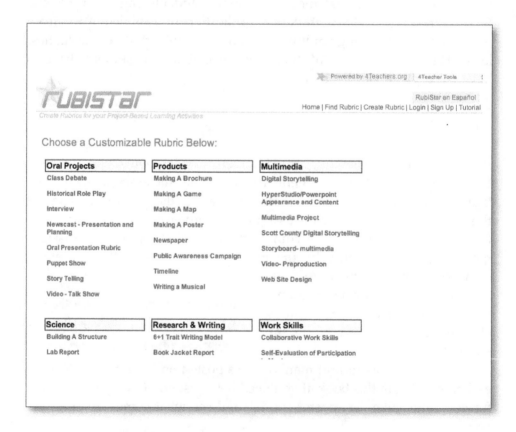

WHAT TO DO WHEN TECHNOLOGY DEVICES ARE LACKING IN YOUR SCHOOLS

If you do not have a set of laptops in your classroom, pair students who have smartphones or tablets with those who do not have them. Between 2011 and 2013, smartphone ownership climbed from 35 percent to 56 percent, with most of those not owning them falling in the senior citizen category. Seventy-nine percent of those in the 18 to 24 age bracket own one. Even in homes making less than $30,000 a year, fully 43 percent of the families have a smartphone (Smith, 2014). Fifty-one percent of high school students are bringing smartphones to school, and fully 25 percent of all K–12 pupils have one with them in their schools (Cavanaugh, 2013). This doesn't even count those that bring iPods and other devices that have Internet accessibility. Indeed, these devices do not need a data plan to be connected to the school's free WiFi, which means parents can purchase smartphones with Internet capability, but they do not have to purchase the data plan.

> Fifty-one percent of high school students are bringing smartphones to school, and fully 25 percent of all K–12 pupils have one with them in their schools.

The good news is that devices are becoming more affordable over time. We are starting to see more and more cloud-based laptops that are coming down in price. For example, Google's Chromebooks retail for $250 or less, and tablets such as the Kindle Fire or the Nexus series all sell for less than $300. Just as students have not minded bringing in smartphones to school, they will not mind doing so with their less expensive tablets and laptops. As pencil, paper, and notebooks have been a normal staple of what parents purchased for their children, tablets or web-based laptops will soon be expected as well. Over time, I have seen some parents of my students purchase Internet devices as a result of my class. It wasn't that the family could not afford the device, but rather than they didn't think it was necessary for school.

Until every student has an Internet-based device, however, find out where the nearest public libraries are and whether your community has youth centers where students can get online access to complete homework assignments. In the meantime, though, schools still need to provide devices for students, and teachers need to be flexible with their deadlines, depending on students' access to the Internet.

To see the links in this chapter, use your smartphone and the QR box below. Alternatively, you can go to http://bit.ly/digitalclassroomteacherguide if you prefer to use your laptop.

CLASSROOM EXAMPLES

Online textbooks come with lots of ancillaries. While you need to log into the book to see the text, you do not need to do so for the ancillaries. For example, my students' online textbook comes with maps, videos, assessments, and more. So in preparing a lesson I might ask my students to read two or three pages in the text; but then, using a Google Drive document, I also link to one of the textbook's maps. Since access to the maps does not require a login and password, the students can click on my link and easily view the map. When my students read about the Great Wall in China, for example, they can read the short description in our text and then look at the linked URL for a map from our ebook. I also have a link to a short Travel Channel video on viewing parts of the Great Wall that few people ever see. By curating a list of links onto a Google Drive document, I can use technology to combine the best of my online textbook with the best of web resources for a richer student interactive.

One of the ways we use online resources in my classroom is to prepare for second-chance tests. In my state, students who narrowly miss passing the state exam (defined as between 375 and 399, where 400 is passing) are given their scores broken down into six individual categories. I create a separate Google Drive document for each of the categories and then have each student work on improving his or her two lowest scores. On the review sheet, I include a very short review video as well as some new review questions that cover only the one particular area identified by the state examiners. You might also consider working with your PLC to cover the first- and second-chance assessments, both in terms of review as well as the assessments themselves. By maximizing their studying of their weakest areas of knowledge, students almost always pass the state exam on their second try. Compare this to the traditional method where students review all of the content covered by the exam for a second-chance test, even if they have already mastered parts of the material.

Rubrics help me even when I am not in the classroom. I often miss the last week of school to grade Advanced Placement exams, but I insist that my students receive the same rigor of instruction even though I am not in the classroom. This year I assigned an essay that explored the connections individual students have to foreign countries. This might mean looking at where their clothes are made, or talking to people in call centers in India, or perhaps researching the country where their parents were born, if one (or both) of their parents are immigrants. For the second part of the assignment, they were asked create an online presentation. The students were given a rubric for both parts of the assignment. We went over the rubric to ensure each student understood the requirements. Then, as each part of the assignment was completed, the students shared it with me via Google Drive. In the evenings, I provided feedback telling them what needed to be improved. They were able to receive feedback from me on how to improve their work (and many of them did), even though I was 2,000 miles away.

A great classroom example of an interactive assignment from outside my school involved one of my neighbor's children. She had been given an assignment to create a Fakebook page for a book she was reading. She was asked to create a page for the main character and then create "friends" for each of the other central characters. She then had to compose a series of conversations between the characters that demonstrated her understanding of the book and the interactions in it. This is a very creative and fun example of how teachers can combine the rigorous levels of Bloom's taxonomy while taking advantage of the new tools offered by the Internet.

EDUCATOR CHALLENGES

Monday Morning Challenge: Using Bloom's taxonomy and Rubistar, develop an interactive assignment that will help your students master some of the content you are covering in class.

Tuesday Morning Challenge: Identify a section of your textbook that does not adequately cover your standards. To supplement the text, provide students with a link to Wikipedia. Find the link(s) to the specific sections of the Wikipedia entry that will be most helpful for your students.

Wednesday Morning Challenge: To help students who have done poorly on an exam, be it the end-of-the-year review or some other significant exam, search Hippocampus to find a video that is targeted to a specific area of weakness. Create a review project based on that video (or videos).

Thursday Morning Challenge: Have a fellow teacher analyze one of your interactive assignments—perhaps one you are using with a flipped video. Ask the teacher to assess what levels of Bloom's taxonomy it covers. If you have missed some of the higher levels you were aiming for, retool your assignment.

Friday Morning Challenge: Give your students the outline of a unit or subunit and have them create an eTextbook collaboratively on Google Drive.

Twitter Hashtag Challenge: Share the link for one of your Google Drive interactive assignments on #individualizelearning.

6

Student Collaboration

Engaging Students With Mobile Learning

- Learn how to make the case for BYOD in the classroom
- Learn how to engage your students with cooperative groups
- Learn about more tools you can use to engage your students

Most of your students now are coming to your classroom with smartphones, iPods, or tablets (if not laptops as well). This chapter will help you see how to integrate these remarkable devices into your instruction.

MAKING THE CASE FOR MOBILE DEVICES IN THE CLASSROOM

In 2013, 37 percent of teens had smartphones, and fully 50 percent used them as their primary devices to access the Internet. Amazingly, this is a 14 percent increase from 2011. Teachers are slowly adapting to the fact that students are more than happy to do their work online. Teachers who are considering placing assignments online can take comfort in the fact that 93 percent of teenagers have access to a computer. The only downside is that 71 percent of users say they share it with one or more family members (Madden, Duggan, Cortesi, & Glasser, 2013). Teens are ever more adept at using their smartphones, sending and receiving, on average, sixty texts a

> Teachers have to repeatedly remind themselves that what worked for them as students is no longer the case for their pupils.

day in 2012 (Lenhart, 2012). Unlike their parents, most teens are quite happy to research and type on their mobile devices. For our purposes, "mobile devices" will be defined as smartphones, iPods, and tablets. But with laptops decreasing in size and people moving more and more toward using detachable keyboards with their tablets, the differences between devices and laptops are starting to blur.

The long and the short of it is that students are not only adept at using online devices, but they have also become an integral part of their daily existence. Teachers have to repeatedly remind themselves that what worked for them as students is no longer the case for their pupils. This is probably more the case for the current generation than for those from the past one hundred years. After all, even your parents' parents used pencils, papers, and books. Now we are looking at a variety of digital devices in the classroom, requiring an entirely different methodology in the way we teach.

Most classrooms in the United States now have access to at least one fairly speedy device that allows users to connect to the Internet; access test-taking software; look up information; compose text on cloud-based documents; and quickly communicate with experts around the world, often in real time. In classrooms where there are a limited number of computers, think how much more could be done if student smartphones, iPods, and so on, could be utilized. Despite the added benefits offered by students' own mobile devices, many teachers and administrators remain reluctant to incorporate them into classroom learning. Many of these same school leaders lament not having enough laptops or tablets to turn their classroom into 21st century learning centers. Instead, students are asked to slog through dull textbooks to find answers they could easily find in seconds by using a smartphone. If you want to individualize your classroom and you need more devices than what the school provides, start with what you have access to (smartphones). Overcoming the device obstacle, allows you the freedom to explore better options for personalizing your students' learning.

Bring Your Own Device (BYOD)

While you may like to teach in a school where every student has a laptop or iPad, it is not always feasible. Enter the BYOD (Bring Your Own Device) trend that is now sweeping schools. BYOD is a way to increase mobile device use in the classroom while not having to foot the considerable costs involved when schools provide one device for every student (also known as 1:1). The Bradford Network's research found that fully 44 percent of

K–12 schools around the United States allow students to bring their own digital devices, and of these schools, more than half are integrating them into the classroom. Among the schools who do not allow digital devices in classrooms, 84 percent have received requests to enact a policy allowing them, but unfortunately fully 62 percent of schools do not have the bandwidth to handle the increased connections to the Internet (Impact of BYOD in Education, 2013).

If you're lucky enough to be working in a school that allows BYOD, it would be ideal if students' devices were allowed, not only in your classroom but also in the library, the lunchroom, other teachers' classrooms, and the hallway so that students never have the excuse that they can't complete their online assignments outside of your classroom. Allowing for lunchroom and hallway use also decreases the need students will feel to text their friends in class.

Changing Teaching Styles in a Digital Classroom

One of the goals of this chapter is to encourage teachers to see the advantage of changing their teaching styles in ways that incorporate mobile devices into instruction in order to further engage students in learning. Consider your class goals. Who should be doing more work in the classroom—the students or the teacher? When students are all working (either individually or in groups) using their devices, there is no front-of-the-room focus. In this scenario, students are charged with being responsible for their own learning. Students (and teachers) have to learn to stay on task by acting as independent agents of their own learning. Teachers encourage staying on task by walking around the room, engaging students by asking and fielding questions and by providing constant formative assessment. Teachers will know that if a student is laughing at his or her screen, she or he is probably not on task. Walking over to the student's desk and hovering nearby usually helps diminish this infraction and reminds students to get back on task without the teacher having to say a word. Finally, require the students to keep their smartphones on their desks. If you are walking around, they will be less inclined to be off task if the devices are easily seen by you.

Another change to consider is including music in the classroom. I fought this trend for years, until my students egged me on long enough to let them try it. What I found was somewhat staggering—students quieted down and got to work. It simply blew me away. It turns out that there is research to back up

> When students are all working (either individually or in groups) using their devices, there is no front-of-the-room focus.

this phenomenon. Dr. Amit Sood's studies have found that soothing music releases dopamine, which rewards the mind. Dr. Theresa Ludnik found that music listeners finished their work faster and were more creative than nonlisteners (Padnani, 2012). You might want to have music playing that the whole class listens to; or you might simply allow students to listen to their own music, provided that they wear earbuds and do not distract their nearest neighbors. Teachers do need to be wary of students who will try to half listen when a teacher is speaking by leaving one earbud in and one out. That will not work! You also will want to strike a deal with the students that they cannot go on YouTube after each song and will have to find a radio channel to listen to that streams a steady playlist of music, so as to minimize the disruption of students seeking out a different song every four minutes. A free site you can suggest to your students is Grooveshark, which has virtually every song and album including the latest releases. My students set their devices on Grooveshark, push the play button, and then get to work without having to think about changing their music after each song. Remember, we are engaging students in the way that suits them best, not necessarily the way we as teachers learn best.

Smartphones can also be useful for

- watching videos, such as your flipped lectures,
- taking notes or working on a project in Google Drive, and
- serving as a quick way to find answers to questions.

The majority of your students will have either Android or Apple devices. Each of these devices can be loaded with applications (or "apps"), which are programs that run on the device. These apps are becoming increasingly more sophisticated and thus more useful tools to use in the classroom. For example, the Google Drive app can be downloaded onto a smartphone or tablet, so that students can work on their Google Drive documents directly from their mobile devices. To get apps for Android devices visit Google Play store, and for Apple devices visit the iTunes store. Since tablets and smartphones have different sizes, developers have to make sure that apps are compatible for both. The truth is that not all apps for smartphones and tablets are as good as the equivalent tool that you can access with a laptop. However, apps have come a very long way in a short period of time and are fast approaching the ability to accomplish the tasks you usually would accomplish on a laptop. Surprisingly, there are even apps that can accomplish tasks not available on their counterpart's web page. Considering that while the iTunes app store started only in 2008, it is pretty remarkable that in its first nine months it provided one billion downloads. As of 2013, there were one million apps that had been collectively downloaded 50 billion times, netting developers $10 billion (Lloyd, 2013). Those kinds of numbers are a powerful incentive for developers to keep creating more and better apps for mobile devices. This is yet another reason why it is important to utilize the resources of your online PLCs to follow educational leaders who are on the cutting edge and who can tell you about new innovations that can have huge impacts on your classroom.

ENGAGING YOUR STUDENTS WITH COOPERATIVE GROUPS

Cloud-Based Cooperative Groups

For group work, students are usually placed into groups of four or five, limited to the students in a given class. However, if you allow students to organize into groups using Google Drive as a platform, you can combine students in one class with students in another, even though the classes meet at different times or on different days. To accomplish their group work, students can communicate with one another using Skype, FaceTime, or Google Hangouts (explained in Chapter 7) for virtual meetings in real time. Most students will come to your classes already experts in using these programs or will easily get the hang of them after one or two attempts. If students are limited to phones that do not have data plans or cannot be connected to WiFi, they can use FreeConferenceCall.com to discuss the assignment with one another outside of class time. FreeConferenceCall does require a login/password, but the teacher can set it up and give the code to groups at their appointed meeting time or just give the numbers to students to decide a meeting time on their own. Each time there is a virtual meeting, you will receive an e-mail after its completion, giving you the ability to monitor who is using the conference calls. No longer do students need to be physically in the same place. This is a decided advantage of using Google Drive tools for group work, as well as the tools available to get together virtually.

International Cooperative Groups

Online Video communication tools can also bring students from multiple continents together. For example, former British Prime Minister Tony Blair started a group called <u>Face to Faith</u> to connect students from around the world. Despite the name, the group barely touches on religion. By visiting the Face to Faith website, teachers can select students from other countries who are the same age as their own students to start a dialogue. If your class is studying Renaissance art, it might be interesting for them to connect with a school in Florence. While you may want to ask the Italian students if they have visited historical sites in their area, the discussion may be as mundane as the students from each country sharing what types of clothes they wear and the food they eat. The benefit of the site is that students are logging into a protected environment. Given the Face to Faith site, or others like it, in addition to cloud-based tools, it is possible to create ongoing collaborative projects with students from other countries. Your students would benefit from getting an insider's perspective on foreign cultures and perhaps a deeper understanding of the topics you are covering in class. Teachers can also use the Face to Faith network to collaborate with teachers from abroad who might be working on a similar content area or related interactive project.

Cooperative Learning Using Twitter

Students live much of their lives online. While they have been leaving Facebook in droves, they are now choosing to spend time on other social networks such as Instagram, Twitter, and more recently, Snapchat (Soper, 2013). As has been stated previously, teachers cannot force students to join these sites without violating FERPA laws, but since many of your older students might already be active on Twitter, they will likely be more than willing to use Twitter for a classroom activity.

Twitter gives you a chance to connect to students for assignments both in and outside of the traditional work day. Twitter brings education to students' more "natural" habitat, often meaning they will be more engaged than with traditional pen and paper assignments. To conduct a "discussion" with Twitter, you will need to create a hashtag (see Chapter 2).

- You might create a hashtag such as "#hallaartclass." If students miss the discussion, they can find it simply by going to the search engine on Twitter and typing in the hashtag.
- When students Tweet a comment, make sure they add the hashtag to their Tweet so that the Tweet is included in the ongoing discussion. Putting the hashtag in the conversation allows everyone to watch the discussion unfold. You can do this either by going to the search engine and entering the hashtag or by using TweetChat or Twitterfall, which will list the Tweets one after the other. Look at the conversation below and you can see the comments both include "#apgovhelp."

- When you are watching conversations with your students, you might remember from Chapter 2 that everyone has a handle, which is their Twitter name preceded by the "@" sign. So, in the example above, my handle is "@kenhalla."
- Just as you are now following others online as part of your growing PLC, students do the same as a way to connect with a large number of friends or celebrities all at once.
- You might, though, tell your students to precede the conversation with "@HideChat" so that only those following the particular hashtag will see the comments, but not all of their friends.

Using a Google Drive Document for Students Not on Twitter

Generally you cannot force a student to join any social networking site not provided by your school district. Therefore, if you would like to use Twitter for an assignment, you will need to provide an alternative for students who do not want to participate on Twitter. One alternative would be to create a Google Drive document where students can post comments and respond to their classmates' comments. The students can now sit at home and have a discussion on Google Drive very similar to one they would have on Twitter.

- On Google Drive, go to the "share" button on the upper right side of the page.
- A new screen will pop up. Beside the words "private access" is the word "change . . . ." Click on "change . . . ."

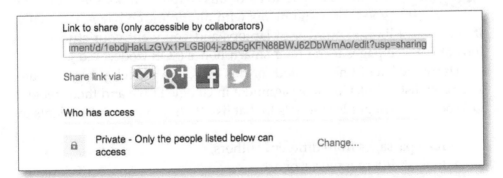

- Another screen will appear. Click on the radio dial beside the words "Anyone with the link."

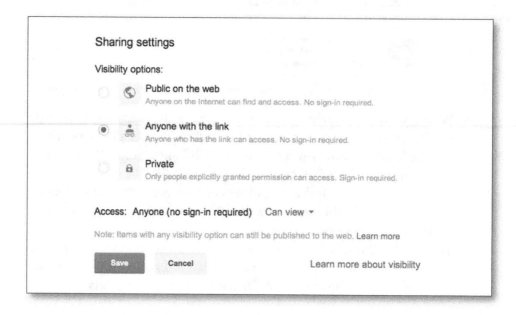

- Then go down to where it says in blue "Can view" near the bottom of the screen, click on the upside-down arrow, and set it to "edit."
- Now copy the URL at the top of the page and give the link to students.
- Now the students without Twitter can have a conversation as well.

OTHER TOOLS TO ENGAGE STUDENTS

Integrating Quick Response Into the Classroom

Another way to incorporate mobile learning in your classroom is to use QR codes, which you have been seeing in each chapter since the beginning of this book. The QR box below takes you to all of this chapter's links. QR codes are good for assignments with multiple web pages, especially if you have a limited number of laptops and you want your students to look at the web pages using their smartphones ("QR Code," n.d.).

Using the list of links created for this book as a model, you can create your own list of links for an assignment in Google Drive and then create a QR code that will guide students to that list. Perhaps you want students to

- read passages from different authors,
- look at different works of art,

- see different video explanations for problem sets, and
- watch historical events.

To create your own QR code, use the following procedure.

- Go to a browser on your laptop and look for a "QR generator." "Kerem Erkan" is one that you might use.
- Copy your URL into the URL box. Note that most generators include "http" in the box, so be sure not to replicate that portion of the web address.
- Click on "Generate code."
- You will be given a unique QR box, which you can either download or copy.
- Paste the QR code into a document and give the document to your students.
- QR codes were generally not designed for laptops, but if yours has a camera, you can Google "QR reader laptop." If you are willing to download a small app, you can use your laptop to read the QR code. Alternatively, as you are creating the QR codes, you can also give your students the equivalent web links so that they have multiple ways of obtaining the information.

Jigsaw Grouping

QR codes can be used to upgrade traditional ways of grouping students, such as jigsaw groups. In jigsaw grouping, you divide a class into four expert groups. Each group reads one of four articles, learns a new concept, or looks at images. The groups then break up and teach the material they have just learned to another newly formed group. Now imagine (and I know this part isn't hard!) that your school does not have enough laptops for each student to access the Google Drive document where links to the images or articles are stored.

- Create a Google Drive document that includes the different QR codes for each article, image, story, and so on, that you might want to use as part of the jigsaw assignment.
- If the items you would like to use are not digitized, then digitize the images by scanning them and uploading the scans into a folder in Google Drive.
- Go to the share link and set the folder to be viewable by anyone with the link.
- Use the QR creator to create a link for your students to access all of the folder's contents. You can even literally cut and paste the QR

boxes onto a piece of paper and hand out the paper to students who will access the links with their smartphones and tablets, therefore getting around the obstacle of there not being enough laptops or computers for each student.

Online Platforms

If you are truly going to move toward a second-order, digitized, student-paced classroom, then you should seriously consider putting your assignments on a social-learning platform such as <u>Blackboard</u>, <u>Edmodo</u>, <u>Moodle,</u> or <u>Google Classroom</u>. These platforms that can be accessed by smartphones and tablets allow teachers to post assignments and videos so students can access their work from anywhere. They also allow teachers to communicate with students within a protected environment. You can access Edmodo and Moodle for free. The aforementioned platforms can be locked down, meaning students can be required to use a login and password. But if you want anyone to see your assignments, you can use a <u>Google Sites</u> account and tailor it for your classroom needs. The benefit of Google Sites is that other educators can see, learn, and borrow your assignments and ideas, not to mention that your students will never forget their logins or passwords (because they are not required).

By placing all of your assignments in one platform, you are creating an environment where students can move effortlessly from one assignment to the next. The online platform can be broken up into units with a folder and subfolders for each individual assignment. Of course, if you really wanted to avoid using a social learning platform altogether, you could just create a Google Drive document and then create links to each assignment from the one document. This would mean that you would start with your first unit and list each of the assignments on the Google Drive document. Then, assuming all of the assignments were online, you could just link from the main page (like a table of contents with hyperlinks) to each assignment.

Texting Student Reminders

Another way to encourage students to be more invested in their school work is to use smartphones to remind them about homework. On a daily basis, my students have to write their homework assignments into their iPods, smartphones, tablets, or paper planners. But I have found that writing them down is not enough for students to remember. So I also text students a reminder at about the same time I believe they should be working on their homework. Is this overkill? Perhaps, but since I started this technique, my students' homework completion has increased significantly.

A very simple remedy for the missing-homework blues is Remind. com. Remind allows you to send your students messages. Keeping FERPA and COPPA in mind (see Chapter 1), you'll need to inform students' parents about the site. The site allows only one-way texting and mandates that a text is sent to at least three students so that there is never a concern for potentially improper texting between a teacher and an individual student. To sign up for the free service, visit Remind.com.

- In the upper left hand side of the page, go to the "Add +" to add a class. Name the class. It might be useful to call it something like "Art ClassAM" for your art class that you have first period.
- On the right side of the page are instructions to tell people how to join. Each class is given a unique code and number that students and parents will text to sign up for reminders.
- Remind will then text them back asking for their name.
- I always have far more people sign up than are in my classes since many parents love to get the reminders as well. Have parents sign up as "Mr./Ms. Last Name" to distinguish between parents and students.

- To send a message, go to the message box (middle of the screen above) and put in your 140-character message. By using the "+" button by the class name, you can send it to multiple classes at once.
- You can also set the time you want a message to go out. I always choose 6:00 p.m., as I assume most students are home from activities and working on homework by that time. If you go to the "Schedule for later" button during the day, you can schedule a message for another time. In addition to homework, I also send students messages

during the school day to coincide with our class changes so they can remember to bring something for class.

- Right beside the scheduling icon, there is a button to use to attach an additional item, in case you want to send your students an attachment at the same time as your message.
- If you want to send a text to a subset of your class, in groups as small as three, once you have clicked on a class, start typing the students' Remind name (e.g., "K Halla") and it will pop up in the "To" box. Then you can remind just a few students about a missing project. At the same time, each of the three students will not know that others have been contacted, so no sensitive information such as missing assignments will be shared.
- If students do not have smartphones, they can select to receive the messages via e-mail as well.

One caution that you will have to think about is that even if you also have students write their homework assignments on their mobile devices, they will become dependent on your texts. If you forget to send a reminder, you will see the number of students not doing homework go up precipitously. If that's the case, you might have to consider giving your students a homework pass rather than charge them with being late. In addition to being able to use the Remind website, you can also download the app for your phone and update it on the fly, in case you remember to remind your students when you are not near a computer. There are other homework reminders available, which you can find by searching the phrase "homework remind text."

Shrinking Your URLs

Occasionally, you might want to include a URL in texts, but a URL is often too long to fit into 140 characters. You might want to write it on the board so students can use their mobile devices to get to a web page or include it in a Remind text. Here are the steps to make this possible.

- Go to tinyurl.com and enter (or copy and paste) the URL in the box. This might be a URL for a Google Drive document that has a very long URL. Press "Make Tinyurl," and it will shrink the very long URL to about 10 characters, which you can then copy and paste into your the texts.
- The advantage of the Tinyurl site is that you can create a unique "Custom alias" URL, which you can use over and over for the same

document. For example, you might want to call your custom alias link "tinyurl.com/hallaclassassignment." Enter "hallaclassassignment" into the box under "Custom alias"; and, if no one has used it before, after pushing your enter key, Tinyurl will tell you that your students can now use this URL. I often use this technique when sharing my assignments with other teachers, as this affords them the ability to write a simple, easy-to-remember link on their whiteboards or easily to e-mail or Tweet it to their students.

While Tinyurl will keep your links for as long as it is a viable company, you will have to write down each or compile them on a cloud-based document to store them. Another shortener that you might consider is Bitly, which will also create unique URLs, but it will store them for you on your home page. You will have to sign up for a free account to save the links, whereas you will not have to do so when using Tinyurl.

- To use Bitly, create an account and then go to the upper right side where it says "Paste a link here."
- A new screen will appear in the center of your computer screen.
- If you want to create a unique name, click on the pencil beside the name to personalize it. Once you have completed creating the link, Bitly will add your new link to the list of your other shortened links.

Visit http://bit.ly/digitalclassroomteacherguide to access live links.

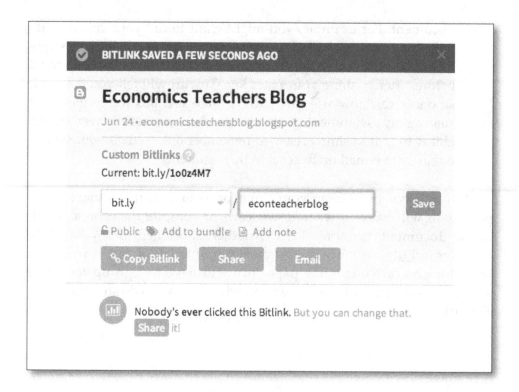

CLASSROOM EXAMPLES

When I started teaching World History, I borrowed a lesson from a friend in which students were asked to look at Byzantine mosaics. The lesson involved placing photocopies of art on the walls of the classroom and having the students walk around to answer a set of questions on a sheet of paper. Using QR codes, I have been able to improve on this lesson. Instead of photocopies, my students now look at digital images of the art on their computers or mobile devices. Most mobile devices allow students to zoom in on any portion of the work to see minute details that would not be possible with photocopies. Additionally, students can find more in-depth information on the work and its history by researching it on the web.

Another way I use QR codes is to create one that links to a Google Drive document listing all classroom assignments. This is useful for students who do not want to write down their homework. I put the most recent assignments at the top of the document so that students do not need to scroll to the bottom of the list to find the most recent assignment. I find that having a list of assignments is incredibly useful to have on hand when a student enters my class midyear. I make a digital copy of the document and then tailor (edit) it for the student, including only enough of the key assignments needed for him or her to catch up. I recently had a student who was in the class only for a month. Using this technique, we created a self-paced document that he used successfully to pass the state exam.

If you want to break students into groups by pooling students from one or more classes, you can do this using a Google Drive document. A colleague, Monte Bourjaily, and I teamed up our Advanced Placement (AP) Government students (seniors) with juniors from the AP US History class to ask the students to consider how to retool Medicare, Social Security, and the US national debt. The goal was for the seniors to introduce the programs to the juniors after each class had taken their AP exams so that the juniors would be better prepared for the following school year. The project had the added benefit of reinforcing the learning for the seniors who were doing the teaching. We put students into groups, but we veered from traditional student groupings by matching students from classes that met during different periods or even on different days of the week.

This was possible because we allowed students to sign up for their groups using Google Drive documents. Each student group then created its own folder and put all of its work into it. My colleague and I stipulated the parameters of the assignment and added that all work products had to be digitized. The work we received was amazing. Students created web pages, made videos, interviewed people, and gave us links and summaries of their findings. Monte and I served as the facilitators, walking around the room helping students with their work. Throughout the project, we checked on their progress and gave feedback so they could make changes and improvements. The work was published online at TeachingHistory.org by a local university where professors enjoyed seeing the cross-curricular collaboration. TeachingHistory.org is funded by the US Department of Education. You can see the results of the students' work by Googling "Crosscurricular Multimedia: AP U.S. History and Govt Classes Collaborate."

> We put students into groups, but we veered from traditional student groupings by matching students from classes that met during different periods or even on different days of the week.

Another way to promote student collaboration is to encourage students to engage with one another in content-related dialogues. Any class, or group of students, can set up a hashtag for help with the coursework or to organize a conversation. The key here is getting buy-in from your students to ensure that a critical mass participates so that you have a successfully robust conversation. If you go to "#usgovclasssou", you will see a 2014 discussion that several educators and I had with our students during President Obama's State of the Union address. Page down to the very beginning of the discussion, and then move up the page to watch the discussion progress. You will see that the several teachers and I added in comments to help the students better understand the State of the Union speech. We even had one of our school board members join in the discussion.

(Continued)

(Continued)

The conversation was so popular, with so many of our students contributing multiple Tweets, that we were trending—meaning we were one of the top ten hashtags in the United States for the second half hour of the speech. Imagine the joy my students felt when they saw that their conversation was in the same national ranking class as the Fox News hashtag. For an assignment where students had to Tweet only three times during the ninety-minute speech, many of our pupils were tweeting from twenty to thirty comments, and doing so long after the school day had ended.

> (Twitter) has the potential to rip down traditional barriers that have kept students in limiting silos where they hear only the opinions of a tiny group of people in their immediate neighborhood and demographic.

The beauty of the hashtag is that students outside of the district can participate in the conversation as well. This has the potential to rip down traditional barriers that have kept students in limiting silos where they hear only the opinions of a tiny group of people in their immediate neighborhood and demographic. Since Tweets remain on Twitter forever, students (from any school) can scroll back through the posts and see comments made weeks or months ago. This may be especially helpful for students who are trying to catch up with the majority of the class because of absence or recent school transfer.

Because Tweets are so public and they remain on the Internet as long as Twitter chooses to keep them there, teachers need to be cognizant of ways to prevent abuse before it occurs. Encouraging responsible digital citizenship and making sure students are aware of what is expected of them are key to ensuring a positive experience for all. What is interesting is that you will see almost no improper language being used precisely because Tweets are visible to the public. Furthermore, school rules still apply in the online environment, meaning that students can face disciplinary action for improper online activity. My students have put up thousands of posts without improper language. When, very rarely, our hashtag is used by people outside of our class, the Tweets have been helpful, so why not embrace that?

Instead of using a hashtag, some teachers ask their students to "tag" them in every post. This means including the teacher's handle in each of their class-related Tweets. My colleague Doug Zywiol uses "@dougzywiol" for his US history students. At the beginning of the 2013–2014 school year, Doug, who had never used Twitter, quickly embraced it as a class warm-up activity. Sure, students could have participated in the warm-up using a daily journal, but they were so much more engaged when entering their warm-up responses on their phones. The exercise was also more interesting for them because they could immediately see the responses of their fellow classmates. The few students without smartphones or iPods were paired up with ones who did have them. Students even voluntarily posted links to items that were relevant to class. So what started as a traditional assignment (class warm-ups) became a way of engaging students long after the class period was over.

EDUCATOR CHALLENGES

Monday Morning Challenge: Choose a television show on Public Broadcasting or an online webcast that you and your students can watch after school hours. Ask students to comment on the program via a Twitter hashtag or a collaborative Google Drive document.

Tuesday Morning Challenge: Set up a Remind page for one of your classes. Share the link with students and parents.

Wednesday Morning Challenge: Create a digital, ongoing, homework assignment page for your students, listing assignments and due dates. Create a QR code for your homework page. Post the QR code somewhere prominent in your classroom.

Thursday Morning Challenge: Create shortened links in Tinyurl or Bitly. Create unique names so your students can easily remember them. Send the unique links using Remind.

Friday Morning Challenge: Set up cooperative student groups between two different teachers' classes. Assign a lesson that will be successful, given the capacities of the two groups.

Twitter Hashtag Challenge: Using #individualizelearning, tell our growing community how you are using mobile devices in the classroom. What alternatives are you offering for students who do not have their own devices? What types of assignments are you using the devices for in class?

7

Formative and Summative Assessment of Student Learning

- Learn how to use technology to create formative and summative assessments
- Learn how to use technology to prepare students for state-run summative assessments
- Learn about technology tools that facilitate virtual meetings of students outside of class

Teachers are being bombarded with local, state, and national standardized tests. Teachers are constantly under the gun to have our students succeed on these tests, even if they are not always the best tools for gauging the learning or achievement of our students. In an ideal world, students would work at their own pace, taking formative assessments along the way and finishing with a summative exam that applies student learning to real-world scenarios.

> In an ideal world, students would work at their own pace, taking formative assessments along the way and finishing with a summative exam that applies student learning to real-world scenarios.

These "tests" would allow students to use their digital devices to solve an open-ended problem, rather than a multiple-choice or essay exam that requires mostly memorization to do well. This is not to say that knowing facts does not have a place in our schools, because students (and adults) do need to have a large number of facts at their disposal. How often, though, are we going to be confronted in life with three or four distinctly wrong choices and only one correct choice? Rather, aren't we more likely to have several choices, any one of which might be a good choice, but none of which is perfect?

FORMATIVE AND SUMMATIVE EVALUATIONS

Before we can delve into formative and summative assessments, teachers will need to decide how quickly to let the students move through the material. For our purposes, formative assessments cover parts of a unit, and summative ones show mastery of the entire unit. Second, teachers have to define what level of mastery they want each student to accomplish by the end of the term. Equally as important is to consider what to do if a student has not reached the defined mastery level by the end of the term or assessment. Finally, teachers have to devise a plan and philosophy for how they will grade students. Consider the various scenarios that might occur regarding student grading and assessment, and think about how you will address them. What if a student is motivated to work ahead of the pace of the class and finishes the class in March? Will that student be allowed to start another course, and should the course continue over the summer break? Will you erase the earlier grades and, instead, substitute the final test score if a student shows mastery on the summative assessment? What if a student does well on all the interactive assignments? Will you let her or him retake the summative test or fix some parts of a project that need work? Will this mean that students will not study the first time if they know they can redo a test? These are all questions that you and your school-based PLC, and perhaps even your school administration, will need to tackle—as the answers will vary from class to class, school to school.

Once these questions are addressed, you can move onto formative and then summative assessments. Often these are thought of as multiple-choice quizzes and exams, as teachers have been conditioned to prepare for state and national exams with those formats. Following the guide of textbooks, teachers often break down units of study into multiple-choice, end-of-unit tests to prepare for the end-of-the-year cumulative assessment. But assessments do not have to always be multiple choice, nor do they even have to be formal. How many times a day does a teacher ask "dipstick" questions of a class and note how many seem eager to answer the questions and how many turn down their heads to avoid eye contact? Even the questions students ask one another and the teacher can indicate formative success or confusion. Students who want more background on a subject probably understand the basics, while those who need a question repeated probably need help with the basic facts. The goal of formative testing is to see where and which students are lacking comprehension. This knowledge can then be used by the teacher either for reteaching purposes or to know when it is time to allow a student to move on to the next part of the unit. That is why it might be a good idea to consider allowing formative assessments to be taken over and over again until the teacher and student are content with the knowledge proficiency. Should students be judged on how long it takes them to learn or instead on how far they have come? Should you be judged on your average ability over the course of your teaching career or on your current level of mastery? Paul Black and his colleagues in their article "Working Inside the Black Box" go as far as to suggest not giving any grades on formative assessments, to avoid student stress (Black, Harrison, Lee, Marshall, & Wiliam, 2004).

Ideally, the goal is for students to be truly prepared to succeed when they come to the end of the unit (summative) exam. The summative exam does not have to be multiple choice. It can be an essay that covers the main parts of the

> Should students be judged on how long it takes them to learn or instead on how far they have come? Should you be judged on your average ability over the course of your teaching career or on your current level of mastery?

unit, a collaborative project, or anything else that registers high on Bloom's taxonomy. For example, for a summative test on our Rome unit, my students read multiple documents, interpreted them, and then integrated the information gleaned from the documents with other learned facts into an essay. My English Speakers of Other Languages (ESOL) especially noted that they learned more from that exercise than any other assignment that year. Why was that? The students had a different document for almost everything we had learned in the unit, and they were forced to think about how all of the different sections were connected. Although it served as a summative assessment, the assignment served the dual purpose of also reinforcing their learning for each aspect of the unit.

At the end of the unit, students are then given summative assessments, which are often referred to as the test for the unit. Many educators give multiple-choice exams, but they need not do this. Instead, they can include student interactive assignments, essays, projects, and so on, that were discussed in Chapter 5. If the work here is superior and adequate mastery is demonstrated, the question a teacher then must consider is whether earlier failures on the unit's materials or formative exams should be discounted. Compare this scenario to children who are learning to play a game online. They fail miserably for weeks before getting to the point where they can easily master the game each time they play. Should they be judged by their failures or by their ultimate success?

Visit http://bit.ly/digitalclassroomteacherguide to access live links.

PREPARING FOR THE FORMATIVE AND SUMMATIVE EVALUATIONS

Unfortunately, not all students know how to or are willing to adequately prepare for a formative or summative assessment. Certainly one hopes that most of the learning has been accomplished through interactive assignments, but some review is almost always necessary. Having students work on a study guide is often helpful, whether it is one you have developed or one that students in a group create with teacher assistance. Then comes the hard part—studying! I encourage my students to get together in groups to quiz each other. This forces them to prepare, so as to not be embarrassed in front of their peers. If they take advantage of the free online tools available, students can study in groups without leaving the comfort of their homes.

Study Groups on Google Hangouts

As we discussed in Chapter 2 on PLCs, you can create a <u>Google Hangout</u> to study with a partner when you are both in different locations. Most of your students have their own Google accounts, and many have been using the Hangouts on their own for fun. Simply suggesting it as an alternative goes a long way toward helping them prepare for the exam. While your students may use FaceTime on Apple products, Hangouts can be used on any device, be it a laptop or smartphone, Apple, or Android. It even works if there is no camera, so long as the students can speak into a mic and hear the other students. Hangouts can even be recorded to be watched by other students via YouTube, should the students on the Hangout choose to make that an option.

When students know that they will be quizzed by a fellow student, it is often incentive enough to get them to study by reviewing projects, notes, and flipped videos beforehand to prepare for the study Hangout. A Hangout need be no different from an in-person get-together, but, rather, is one that can more easily accommodate different schedules and transportation issues. Study sessions need be no more innovative than one student asking questions of two or three other peers.

Study Groups on Free Conference Call

You could also suggest FreeConferenceCall.com, which allows your students to engage in a conference call with as many of their friends as they want. This also lets students without an Internet connection join in the fun! One student does have to sign up for the free service, but the only inconvenience is receiving an e-mail after each use.

ONLINE TOOLS FOR CONDUCTING FORMATIVE ASSESSMENTS

Twitter

Use Twitter as a way to check for understanding and to generate classroom discussion. When your students enter the class, Tweet a series of questions and have your students answer them. If the majority of students answer quickly, correctly, and without difficulty, you know that they have mastered the material. However, if they have difficulty with the question, you know that you'll need to review the material before moving on. Your students can also use Twitter to prepare for exams by posting their own questions to a hashtag and having anyone in the class (or for that matter anyone on Twitter) answer the question. Twitter can be a study session that never ends.

TodaysMeet

If you want your students to answer questions in unison during a class using a smartphone, tablet, or web page, you can also use TodaysMeet. It is similar to Twitter, except that there is no signup required. Unless the teacher makes the unique URL public, no one else will see your class discussions. So you could present a question to your students, and they would be able to answer exactly as they do in Twitter—but in a protected place. As with Twitter, the students would see a stream consisting of one comment after another, and you will see (using either Twitter or TodaysMeet) that the quieter students are much less reluctant to start talking in this less intimidating environment. To start a discussion stream, go to the website and follow this procedure.

- Enter in a name for the session, such as "Hallaclassroom," and how long you want it to last, which can be an hour, day, month, and so on. If no one else is using that name, a green checkmark will appear. The new name will be part of the link that you give your students. In the example above, the entire link would be "todaysmeet.com/ Hallaclassroom."
- TodaysMeet is different from Twitter in both its look as well as the fact that others outside of your class cannot join in the discussion. You can save TodaysMeet untouched as long as you want to, whereas on a Twitter hashtag, others can enter into the discussion long after your formal meeting has ended. TodaysMeet is also a great resource for younger students since most of them do not have Twitter.

Visit http://bit.ly/digitalclassroomteacherguide to access live links.

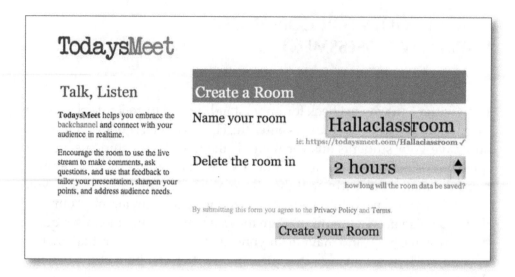

Google Forms and Flubaroo

Yet another way to create a formative quiz is to prepare a Google Drive form. As you know from Chapter 3, anytime you create a Google Form, a spreadsheet is instantly generated of the responses entered. Thus you can quickly scan through the answers, or even spot check them if it is a formative evaluation. Once you have set up the quiz, you can use it again and again by simply deleting the old answers in the generated spreadsheet to wipe out previous student responses.

However, if you would like to set up a way to grade a quiz easily on Google Forms, that will take a bit of time, and it lies beyond the scope of this book. If you are comfortable learning on your own, conduct a search for Flubaroo. Flubaroo is a script that runs a program that is added to your Google Form page. It allows you to add some commands to perform basic instructions, among which will be to tally the points you might have for a simple formative quiz. If you perform a Google search for "Flubaroo tutorial to make a test," you will find several how-to videos to help you out.

Poll Everywhere

Another cool app is PollEverywhere.com. Teachers know it is important to constantly check-in with students to see if they have learned a recently taught concept. Poll Everywhere allows your students to view a set of multiple-choice or free response questions, which they can respond to by texting. Students' responses populate in real time on the teacher's computer screen, which can be projected onto the screen for the whole class to see. This allows the teacher to see right away what, if anything, needs to be retaught. What a great way to give a formative assessment and know instantly what items need reteaching. For students who are using computers rather than mobile devices, you can give them a short URL so they can participate.

- To set up the account, go to the Poll Everywhere site and create your own account.
- Go to "Create a poll" and, in the box that appears, enter in the questions, one after the other.
- It can be as easy as entering the question, followed by commas and the different answer choices. Alternatively, you can select "Open Ended" or "Multiple Choice" and, if it is the latter, you can put the answers on a separate line for each answer.
- Remember that Poll Everywhere is not scoring, so there is no need to put in the correct answers.
- You can also add photos by saving them to your desktop (right click on the photo and go to "Save as"). Then hit the camera icon on the right side of the Poll Everywhere question and upload the image to the question.

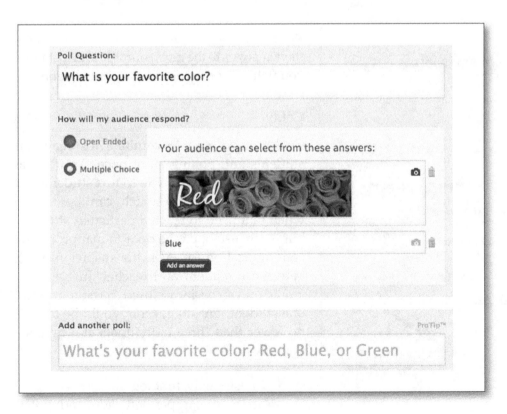

Poll Everywhere will create numbers and codes for your students to text. In the graphic above, for example, students would text "15173" to the number "22333" if they feel that "Definitely" is the correct answer.

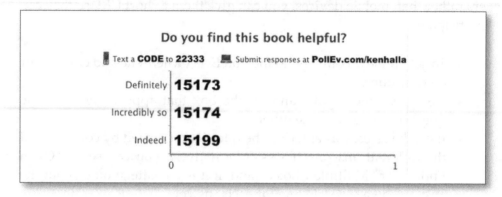

Once you have created the poll, you have several options.

- You can download it as a PowerPoint.
- You can get a URL for a web page link: "How People Can Respond" > "Web devices on," and you will see a short URL.
- You can hide the results from the students so they will not be biased in their choices.

When you begin the poll, students will text their answers to the given number and instantly you will see if they need more remediation.

Cel.ly

Cel.ly allows you to combine texting your students and polling all at once. An item of caution: Cel.ly allows you to text students on an individual basis, which can be useful when you need to reach a particular student; but it can also open the door to inappropriate communication (or even the suspicion of it) between a student and teacher. Just as you would never be in a closed classroom with one student, my suggestion would be to text no fewer than three individuals at a time so you always have a "witness."

- To use Cel.ly, first log in.
- Go to the upper left side and press "Start a cell."

- Decide if you want a curated chat, where messages can be sent only to you, or whether you want students to be able to text back and forth, with everyone seeing all of the messages. Either way, Cel.ly enables students to receive instant feedback outside of class be it from the teacher or the student, but since everything can be seen by you, students will be sure to follow classroom etiquette.
- Either you can choose to send a public link, which you can preset with a password so only your students are allowed in; or you can send students a "golden ticket," which allows anyone with the link to join directly.
- If you want to send poll question(s) to your students, at the top of your cell you will see "New message," which will allow you to send a message or poll (test) question to your students. You can add an attachment or picture.
- Within seconds, you will receive messages back from your students. If a significant number of students do not answer correctly, you can provide web page URLs to help them review the material. This is formative testing on the go! To make sure that students master the material eventually, it is important to follow up with them after they have had some further study time.

Quizlet

Another great site for reviewing material is Quizlet. Because of FERPA and COPPA, school systems will often frown on the practice of mandating the use of sites that require a student login and password. One of the nicest things about Quizlet, however, is that you can use other people's flashcards without either you or your students even joining. If you do join the free site, you can make copies of other people's work and then tailor it for your students' learning.

- To find a set of flashcards, go to "Search Quizlet" at the top of any page.
- You can then tap on "Copy" or, if it is not on your screen, you will find it under "More Tools."

Visit http://bit.ly/digitalclassroomteacherguide to access live links.

- You can then easily edit the cards by writing in the appropriate spaces.
- If you want to create a set of cards from scratch, you just tap on "Create a Set" at the top of any page, and a screen such as the image below will appear. For each new word you want to add, just hit "Add a row" at the bottom of the page and add in the word and the definition.

Here is where the great fun begins. Take the URL for the study cards and link it to your school platform or use Tinyurl or Bitly to give the short link to your students. You could even send it to them using Remind. Now your students can choose to use the traditional flashcards or they can use one of the many games. You can choose Space Race, where knowing the correct answer will destroy the definition traveling across the screen. Alternatively, you can play Scatter, take a test, or make several other choices.

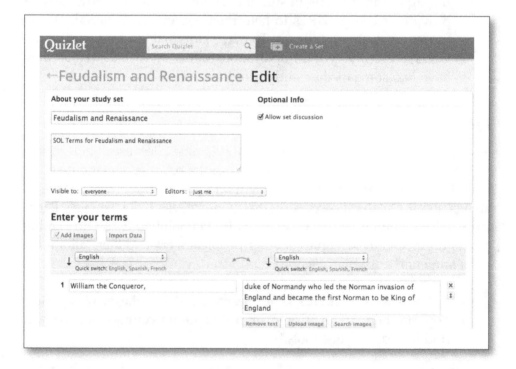

To find hyperlinks for all of the resources mentioned in this chapter, click on the QR box below or visit http://bit.ly/digitalclassroomteacherguide.

CLASSROOM EXAMPLES

If the aim of teaching is to make sure the students have learned, then formative quizzes are a good way to gauge learning. Find a unit review in Quizlet and have your students choose one of the methods they will use to complete the review. My son's teacher likes to set up Space Race and then see who can finish the quickest without missing anything. My son will play each review game over and over, just so he can have class bragging rights. And, yes, he learns the material so much better than if he just went over it once.

The items in this chapter do not have to be limited just to students. I teach a number of technology integration classes for teachers, and I like to get them to see the virtues of using smartphones in

> My son will play each review game over and over, just so he can have class bragging rights. And, yes, he learns the material so much better than if he just went over it once.

class. To that end, I like to finish with a Poll Everywhere exercise, which both shows me how well I did as a teacher of teachers and, more subtly, shows the educators great ways to connect with students.

Another point to note is that one of the teachers in my technology classes loves to use Cel.ly. She will text about ten review questions the night before any test and see how well they do. I asked her to poll her students in front of some educators I was leading, and within fewer than five minutes, twenty of her students responded to her question. Normally she focuses on the big topics. If a particular topic is lagging in positive results, she will text her students a link with relevant information to review.

Finally, one of the colleagues, with whom I teach on a daily basis, likes to use TodaysMeet while he is having his students watch ten- to twenty-minute video clips. Certainly there is no great way to ensure students are watching longer clips such as this, but he finds that students can both watch and write at the same time. From time to time, he sends me a link so I can "watch" his class live, and I am always impressed with how much they are picking up.

EDUCATOR CHALLENGES

Monday Morning Challenge: Find a set of flashcards in Quizlet and give the URL to your students to prepare for the next summative exam. Ask students to study the flashcards in groups you've created. Give students the option of studying together either in person or online.

Visit http://bit.ly/digitalclassroomteacherguide to access live links.

Tuesday Morning Challenge: Set up a TodaysMeet and use it for an at-home discussion. I guarantee your students' parents will want to jump into the discussion!

Wednesday Morning Challenge: With your PLC, develop a nontraditional summative "test" such as an essay, a painting project, a skit, or a presentation. Use Rubistar to create a rubric. Then have your PLC agree to use both the assessment and the rubric as a culminating exercise.

Thursday Morning Challenge: Introduce your students to Google Hangouts and Freen Conference Call before your first test. Put links for both in your student platform under a section titled "Collaborating in the cloud." Ask them to try using one or the other (or both) to study together for the test.

Friday Morning Challenge: Sit down with the technology guru in your school and go to the site Flubaroo and see if the two of you can create a formative quiz for your students.

Twitter Hashtag Challenge: Share your favorite websites for formative and summative evaluations on #individualizelearning.

8

Looking Forward Into the Present

- Briefly review the major topics that were covered in this book
- Put the changes necessary in our school system in context with the changing world
- Highlight a school system that has embraced second-order digital learning

This book has shown over and again that our schools need to change. To some degree, most of our schools have changed little from the Prussian model. Generally all six-year-olds can be counted on to be matriculating into first grade. We still largely teach subjects from kindergarten to college in mini, one-room schoolhouses, where subjects are taught in content vacuums with little collaboration or connection to other classes. On one hand, teachers have embraced Professional Learning Communities where content specialists collaborate on lesson plans and assessments. On the other hand, few schools have progressed beyond basic, cross-curricular models, such as English and history classes matching books to a historical timeline. Rare are the post-elementary schools that connect all learning together. Why is this? We are no longer producing a majority of workers for the assembly line or to manage those in factories. The Internet age has eradicated the need for this model of education. We need a new educational model that embraces

> We need a new educational model that embraces student-centered learning and allows for our pupils to work at their own pace.

student-centered learning and allows for our pupils to work at their own pace. In an increasingly connected world, it is no longer feasible for educators to resist allowing students to use digital devices in the classroom when those devices can help teachers and students achieve the goals of collaboration, exploration, and independence.

To meet the incredibly expensive mandate of providing devices to all of our students, many schools are embracing the practice of BYOD. Some innovative schools are loaning out devices to lower-income students to take home, and many Internet providers are offering reduced prices for home Internet access for these pupils (Dampier, 2011). Since it takes time to adjust to a paperless or individualized Internet-based classroom, teachers must be implementing Internet-based assignments now rather than waiting until most or all of their students have devices of their own to use.

In this book, you have read about the many strategies and tools available that will help you transform your classroom into one that embraces the latest technology, second-order change, deeper levels of learning, and individualized instruction tailored to each student's unique pace. In order to implement the latest curricula and to prepare students for the careers of tomorrow, teachers can no longer remain hidden, speaking behind a podium. Flipping the classroom is one option that will allow teachers to spend more time moving from group to group and from student to student, helping with individualized needs and providing more one-on-one attention to ensure that students are learning and achieving to their highest potential. Consider how much you have learned about your content area since beginning your teaching career. This was not done by memorizing but rather by preparing presentations, creating innovative assignments, and devising assessments for students. The repetition, research, and the thought put into these tasks is what entrenched your mastery of your subject matter and your teaching craft. Your own personal experience as a learner is one of the best arguments for ditching the lectures and, instead, assigning interactive projects for your students to engage them in deeper learning.

Change is happening at a faster and faster pace. Most people bank online, reserve library books virtually, find their travel tickets using multiple websites, and even read their daily news online in multimedia formats. It makes sense to take advantage of the most up-to-date tools available to engage students and guide them in ways to collaborate and create work products that weren't possible with yesterday's technology.

Just as smartphones have become affordable and widespread in recent years, laptops such as Chromebooks and tablets are dropping in price and will soon be ubiquitous in our schools. Keep an eye out for other devices that will soon be appearing in your classroom. Google is testing out "Google Glass," which is a set of glasses with a camera on the upper right side. Users can take pictures or videos by tapping the side of the glasses. Google Glass, via voice commands, can also access websites that the users view through the frames, right in front of their eyes. Think smartphone, but in a hands-free format. Apple, Samsung, and others have now introduced new "computer watches." How might this change impact your classroom? Will it be the next device banned in schools or will it, like the smartphone, lead to a wave of new innovation in your classroom? This book should already have helped you with some tools to fine-tune your teaching to meet the differing needs of your students. Take advantage of the tools mentioned here to allow students to work at their own pace, to reteach lessons when necessary, and to grant students the time to adequately learn the material and therefore find more success in the classroom. But don't wait long! Some teachers and schools are already diving in headfirst!

> Most people bank online, reserve library books virtually, find their travel tickets using multiple websites, and even read their daily news online in multimedia formats. It makes sense to take advantage of the most up-to-date tools available to engage students and guide them in ways to collaborate and create work products that weren't possible with yesterday's technology.

CLASSROOM EXAMPLE: MOORESVILLE, NORTH CAROLINA

One school district that has garnered national attention recently is Mooresville Graded School District in North Carolina. Its superintendent, Mark Edwards, was named the 2013 American Association of School Administrators' Superintendent of the Year because of the amazing transformation made by the school district. Even though the school district is 99th (out of 115) in state funding, its scores are now number two in the state. Graduation rates have improved from 64 percent to 91 percent, compared to the 80 percent state average. Third-grade reading scores have gone up to 94 percent, with Hispanics and African Americans coming in at 91 percent and 92 percent. Math scores for the same age bracket are also in the mid-90s. These changes have come at a time when poverty rates in the district have increased 25 percent and fully 40 percent of the students are on the free or reduced-price lunch program (Campbell, 2012; "Pearson Congratulates," 2013).

Visit http://bit.ly/digitalclassroomteacherguide to access live links.

How did Mooresville increase its test scores and graduation rates so much? It did so by using technology in an interactive way. Superintendent Edwards shifted from buying textbooks for every student to leasing laptops for every teacher and every student from third grade through high school. Laptops were nothing new to Edwards, who gave them to every student when he was the superintendent of Henrico County in Virginia in 2003. The laptops cost $215 a year and were financed in part by increasing class size (Schwartz, 2012). Discipline, though, in larger classes, can be easier if students are involved in interactive learning. Therefore discipline has not been a concern for Mooresville. Let students put in their ear buds and engage them with innovative learning ideas, and the level of retention will go up.

Edwards asked for teachers to have confidence in his idea that they needed to be facilitators, not passive lecturers. They ditched textbooks and replaced them with learning platforms. These can be a variety of things such as interactive assignments, teacher-made textbooks, or completely digitized classes using platforms purchased from a variety of companies. Edwards also gave teachers technology so they could give summative assessments every four and a half weeks and track results on their computers. These assessments gave teachers the ability to target precise problems with each student. Teachers were able to differentiate instruction rather than disseminate one-size-fits-all fixes as had been done in the past. One of the high school teachers even taught his students to be technicians, so smaller technology problems have been fixed for little to no money. Teacher David Sherrill has said that giving students the job of technician has instilled in them leadership as well as confidence (Campbell, 2012).

> These assessments gave teachers the ability to target precise problems with each student. Teachers were able to differentiate instruction rather than disseminate one-size-fits-all fixes as had been done in the past.

Edwards began slowly by first giving laptops to teachers for two years before providing them for students. He also had the foresight to offer teachers summer enrichment courses so that they would be better prepared to provide interactive teaching. Working with the community, Edwards initially secured money from Lowe's Home Improvement store, which has its home office in the town. But he went further, convincing the town to put WiFi in public places like the library, parks, and all public facilities. He also worked to get discounts for Internet access in the homes of students whose families had not been able to afford it in the past (Farrell, 2013).

Mooresville has succeeded by realizing that technology can allow teachers to implement second-order changes that involve teachers' becoming facilitators who provide more individualized student instruction. The proof is in the pudding! For those who believe in the importance of summative testing via state exams, Mooresville's remarkable rise up North Carolina's ranks shows that technology and its enhanced capabilities can lead to better learning, understanding, and classrooms where students feel more successful.

But no one is asking you to change an entire district—although that would be great. One way to make a positive step in the right direction would be to take on the Educator Challenges in this book. Reading this book once will not suffice, you will need to go back and reread sections where you need more help and to look beyond the book to search out more ideas.

Best of luck with your new classroom!

EDUCATOR CHALLENGES

Monday Morning Challenge: Depending on your role in your school, draft a series of goals you would like to set for yourself in the next year to integrate technology into the classroom. Work with your administration to secure funding, and find some avant-garde teachers in your district who would be willing to work through problems that might arise. The teachers do not have to be in the same content area, but they do have to be willing to undertake a new challenge and meet on a regular basis to talk through challenges.

Tuesday Morning Challenge: With your goals above outlined, what are one or two you can reasonably start working on in the next few weeks? Perhaps you could work on one flipped video and an accompanying interactive assignment.

Wednesday Morning Challenge: Once you have completed one interactive assignment, discuss it with your PLC and, if possible, with other forward-thinking collaborators, and decide if any changes will be needed for the next time. Plan out a unit where you can completely integrate technology into your students' curriculum. Work with at least one other teacher so you can support each other.

Thursday Morning Challenge: Seek out the members of your department and teach them two or three things you have learned from this book.

Friday Morning Challenge: Figure out what challenges your students face in terms of obtaining access to the Internet outside of school hours. Research alternatives such as local libraries and youth centers. Talk to your administration about opening up a computer lab after school hours at your school site.

Twitter Hashtag Challenge: What do you think about Mooresville? Are you doing similar things in your school district? If not, what are your hurdles? Share your thoughts on #individualizelearning so our community of educators can work with you to offer you ideas and suggest resources.

References

Bergmann, J., & Sams, A. (2012). *Flip your classroom: Reach every student in every class every day*. Eugene, OR: International Society for Technology in Education.

Berrett, D. (2012, February 19). How 'flipping' the classroom can improve the traditional lecture. *The Chronicle of Higher Education*. Retrieved from http://chronicle.com/article/How-Flipping-the-Classroom/130857/

Black, P., Harrison, C., Lee, C., Marshall, B., & Wiliam, D. (2004). Working inside the Black Box: Assessment for learning in the classroom. *Phi Delta Kappan, 86,* 8–21. Retrieved from http://pdk.sagepub.com/content/86/1/8.full.pdf+html

Bloom's digital taxonomy wheel and knowledge dimension. (n.d.). *EducTechalogy.* Retrieved June 2013 from http://eductechalogy.org/swfapp/blooms/wheel/engage.swf

Bort, J. (2013, October 2). Watch out Microsoft: 22% of all U.S. school districts are using Chromebooks, Google VP says. *Business Insider*. Retrieved from http://www.businessinsider.com/22-percent-us-school-districts-use-chromebooks-2013-10

A brief history of the Internet. (n.d.). *Online Library Learning Center*. Retrieved May 7, 2013, from http://www.usg.edu/galileo/skills/unit07/internet07_02.phtml

Browser statistics. (n.d.). *w3schools.com.* Retrieved July 19, 2013, from http://www.w3schools.com/browsers/browsers_stats.asp

Campbell, T. (2012, October 7). Viewpoint: How Mooresville is effectively teaching every child, every day. *Charlotte Observer*. Retrieved on July 12, 2013, from http://www.charlotteobserver.com/2012/10/04/3577649/how-mooresville-is-effectively.html

Cavanaugh, S. (2013, May 2). Smartphones a standard for majority of students by high school, survey finds. *Education Week*. Retrieved from http://blogs.edweek.org/edweek/DigitalEducation/2013/05/more_than_half_of_students_car.html

Censer, M. (2011, August 27). After dramatic growth, Ashburn expects even more data centers. *The Washington Post*. Retrieved from http://www.washingtonpost.com/business/capitalbusiness/after-dramatic-growth-ashburn-expects-even-more-data-centers/2011/06/09/gIQAZduLjJ_story.html

Dampier, P. (2011, November 9). Low income $9.95 Internet coming to Time Warner, Cox, and Charter . . . if you qualify. *Stop the Cap!* Retrieved from http://stopthecap.com/2011/11/09/low-income-9-95-internet-coming-to-time-warner-cox-and-charter-if-you-qualify/

Data Centers Canada. (2011, February 28). *How does the Internet work?* [Video]. Retrieved from http://www.youtube.com/watch?v=i5oe63pOhLI

Digital citizenship: Using technology appropriately. (n.d.). *Resources.* Retrieved on September 25, 2013, from http://www.digitalcitizenship.net/Resources.html

Farrell, E. F. (2013, Spring). "10 Lessons from the best district in the country." *Scholastic.* Retrieved from http://www.scholastic.com/browse/article.jsp?id=3757944

Felder, R. M., & Silverman, L. K. (1988). Learning and teaching styles in engineering education. *Engineering Education, 75,* 674–681. Retrieved from http://www4.ncsu.edu/unity/lockers/users/f/felder/public/Papers/LS-1988.pdf

Fredericks, A. (n.d.). Lesson methodologies. *Teacher Vision.* [Excerpted from Anthony D. Fredericks, *The complete idiot's guide to success as a teacher,* 2005, Alpha Books.] Retrieved June 2013 from http://www.teachervision.fen.com/curriculum-planning/teaching-methods/48355.html

Frishberg, D. (1975). *Schoolhouse Rock: I'm just a bill* [Video]. Retrieved July 24, 2014, from https://www.youtube.com/watch?v=FFroMQlKiag

Grathwohl, C. (2011, September 23). Wikipedia comes of age. *The Chronicle of Higher Education.* Retrieved from http://chronicle.com/article/article-content/125899/

Greaves, T., Hayes, J., Wilson, L., Gielniak, M., & Peterson, R. (2010). The technology factor: Nine keys to student achievement and cost-effectiveness. Project RED, MDR [publishing partners]. Retrieved from http://pearsonfoundation.org/downloads/ProjectRED_TheTechnologyFactor.pdf

History of the Internet. (n.d.). *Wikipedia.* Retrieved May 7, 2013, from http://en.wikipedia.org/wiki/History_of_the_Internet

How to use Twitter to grow your PLN. (2012, December 7). *Edutopia.* Retrieved from http://www.edutopia.org/blog/twitter-expanding-pln

The impact of BYOD in education. (n.d.). *Bradford Networks.* Retrieved November 24, 2013, from http://www.bradfordnetworks.com/impact_of_byod_on_education_survey

Is your birthday an advantage in school? Malcolm Gladwell thinks it is. (2008, December 2). *Education Innovation.* Retrieved from http://educationinnovation.typepad.com/my_weblog/2008/12/is-your-birthday-an-advantage-in-school-malcolm-gladwell-thinks-it-is.html

Khan Academy. (n.d.). *Wikipedia.* Retrieved July 27, 2013, from http://en.wikipedia.org/wiki/Khan_Academy

Khan Academy founder heralds nation's first statewide pilot in Idaho. (2013, February 28). *J.A. and Kathryn Albertson Foundation.* Retrieved from http://www.jkaf.org/khan-academy-founder-heralds-nations-first-statewide-pilot-in-idaho

Lage, M. J., Platt, G. J., & Treglia, M. (2000). Inverting the classroom: A gateway to creating an inclusive learning environment." *The Journal of Economic Education, 31,* 30–43. Retrieved from http://www.tandfonline.com/toc/vece20/31/1

Lenhart, A. (2012, May 19). Teens, smartphones & texting. *Pew Research Internet Project.* Retrieved from http://www.pewinternet.org/Reports/2012/Teens-and-smartphones.aspx

Lloyd, C. (2013, July 10). iTunes App Store turns 5: A look back on 50 billion downloads. *SlashGear.* Retrieved from http://www.slashgear.com/tags/itunes-store/

Madden, M., Duggan, M., Cortesi, S., & Glasser, U. (2013, March). Teens and technology 2013. *Pew Research Internet Project.* Retrieved from http://www.pewinternet.org/2013/03/13/teens-and-technology-2013/

Miller, R. (2012, March 14). Estimate: Amazon cloud backed by 450,000 servers." *Data Center Knowledge.* Retrieved from http://www.datacenterknowledge.com/archives/2012/03/14/estimate-amazon-cloud-backed-by-450000-servers/

Nolen, S. B. (2011). The role of educational systems in the link between formative assessment and motivation, *Theory Into Practice, 50,* 319–326 Retrieved from http://dx.doi.org/10.1080/00405841.2011.607399

Noonoo, S. (2012, June 20). Flipped learning founders set the record straight. *The Journal.* Retrieved from http://thejournal.com/articles/2012/06/20/flipped-learning-founders-q-and-a.aspx

Pariser, E. (2011). *The filter bubble: What the Internet is hiding from you.* New York, NY: Penguin.

Pearson congratulates Dr. Mark Edwards of Mooresville, NC as nation's Superintendent of the Year. (2013, February 22). *Pearson Always Learning.* Retrieved from http://www.pearsoned.com/pearson-congratulates-dr-mark-edwards-of-mooresville-nc-as-nations-superintendent-of-the-year

Posner, J. (2014, May 22). *How a bill really becomes a law: What Schoolhouse Rock missed* [Video]. Vox. Retrieved from http://www.youtube.com/watch?v=QH0Hl31vdF4

QR code. (n.d.). *Wikipedia.* Retrieved October 27, 2013, from http://en.wikipedia.org/wiki/QR_code

Schwartz, A. (2012, February 12). Mooresville's shining example (It's not just about the laptops). *The New York Times.* Retrieved from http://www.nytimes.com/2012/02/13/education/mooresville-school-district-a-laptop-success-story.html?pag

Security and privacy of cloud computing. (2013, January 23). Consortium for School Networking, EdTextNext report. Retrieved from http://www.cosn.org/about/news/cosn-issues-new-report-%E2%80%98security-and-privacy-cloud-computing%E2%80%99

Smith, C. (2014, September 22). How many people use 700 of the top social media, Apps and Digital Services? *Digital Market Ramblings.* Retrieved from http://expandedramblings.com/index.php/resource-how-many-people-use-the-top-social-media/4/#.UxIRQeNdWSo

Soper, T. (2013, May 22). Report: Teens leave Facebook for Twitter, because they want less drama. *GeekWire.* Retrieved from http://www.geekwire.com/2013/pew-report-teens-facebook-twitter-instagram

Spencer, D. (n.d.). Flipped learning resources. Retrieved May 20, 2013, from https://docs.google.com/document/d/1IOI5-tXZvOEVCFhoN5hlsccnRa-8_77nx3GDdB6C-tE/edit

Statistics. (n.d.). *YouTube.* Retrieved October 27, 2013, from http://www.youtube.com/yt/press

Sterling, B. (1993, February). Short history of the Internet. *Internet Society.* Retrieved from http://www.internetsociety.org/internet/what-internet/history-internet/short-history-internet

Sullivan, D. (2013, February 11). Google still world's most popular search engine by far, but share of unique searchers dips slightly. *Search Engine Land.* Retrieved from http://searchengineland.com/google-worlds-most-popular-search-engine-148089

Why does Wikipedia work? (2014, July 30). *Ted Radio Hour* [Audio]. National Public Radio. Retrieved from http://www.npr.org/player/v2/mediaPlayer.html?action=1&t=1&islist=false&id=191625835&m=200479121

Wolchover, N. (2011, January 24). How accurate is Wikipedia?" *Live Science*. Retrieved from http://www.livescience.com/32950-how-accurate-is-wikipedia.html

World Science Festival. (2012, June 3). *There and back again: A packet's tale. How does the Internet work?* [Video]. Retrieved from http://worldsciencefestival.com/videos/there_and_back_again_a_packets_tale

Index

A SAGE Company

Corwin is committed to improving education for all learners by publishing books and other professional development resources for those serving the field of PreK–12 education. By providing practical, hands-on materials, Corwin continues to carry out the promise of its motto: **"Helping Educators Do Their Work Better."**

CPSIA information can be obtained
at www.ICGtesting.com
Printed in the USA
LVHW101632270520
656715LV00006B/360

9 781483 344683